THE
LIFE-CHANGING
MAGIC
OF SHEDS

THE
LIFE-CHANGING
MAGIC
OF SHEDS

Henry Cole

Written with Tom Sykes

Quercus

First published in Great Britain in 2020 by

Quercus Editions Ltd
Carmelite House
50 Victoria Embankment
London EC4Y 0DZ

An Hachette UK company

A CIP catalogue record for this book is available
from the British Library

HB ISBN 978 1 52940 655 9
Ebook ISBN 978 1 52940 657 3

10 9 8 7 6 5 4 3 2

Typeset by CC Book Production
Printed and bound in Great Britain by Clays Ltd, Elcograf S.p.A.

Papers used by Quercus Editions Ltd are from well-managed forests
and other responsible sources.

To my darling wife Janie,
for 28 years of understanding that retiring
to my shed makes me a better husband and
father to our boys, Charlie and Tom!

Contents

THE SHED
COMMANDMENTS

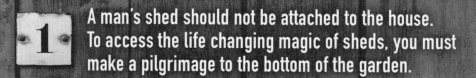

1 A man's shed should not be attached to the house. To access the life changing magic of sheds, you must make a pilgrimage to the bottom of the garden.

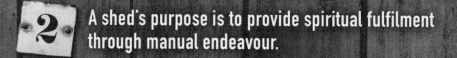

2 A shed's purpose is to provide spiritual fulfilment through manual endeavour.

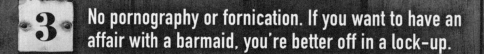

3 No pornography or fornication. If you want to have an affair with a barmaid, you're better off in a lock-up.

4 Wi-Fi is okay, but use it wisely: social media's clamour for validation and approval is everything shed dwellers stand against. Sheds are spaces to dream, to reach the impossible star, but their currency is the nuts and bolts of reality, not fuzzy-brained Instagram positivity.

5   A shed should not have a bed or a toilet. That's not a shed. It's a rubbish house, and can potentially be weaponized in the event of marital discord.

6   Making mistakes in a shed is a good thing, because a man only learns and grows through mistakes.

7   Legal, tax, planning and building regs: all good points. One way or another, your shed probably infringes all of them but you are a blunt-fingered, salt of the earth iconoclast with no time for book learning or thumb-sucking jobsworths. Let them burn. Well, in spirit anyway.

8   Entry to the shed is by invite only. Visitors are welcome, but they should leave with the impression that they have either delayed or assisted great work.

9   TCP (Two Cup Protocol): Only two cups are needed per shed, one for you and one for a visitor. TCP avoids a build-up of dirty cups; in your shed you are an ambassador for the best in humanity, relentless in your pursuit of quiet mastery, not a teenager who can't tidy up.

10   There is no higher compliment one man can pay another than this: 'Do you want to come and see my shed, mate?'

1:
Welcome to Heaven

My shed is my refuge. It's the place where I go when I need a break from this mad, crazy world that, as far as I can tell, just keeps getting madder and crazier.

Mindfulness is very hip now, isn't it? There is no shortage of books, DVDs and podcasts telling you how to chill out, but the way I see it, these are just transient aspirations towards wellbeing. Because when it comes to truly finding out who you are and what makes you tick, there is one thing that's staring you straight in the face, and it needs no online subscription to a cloud-based server with a password you keep forgetting.

That, my friend, is a shed.

But, as per Commandment One, the shed can only help you if it's not attached to the house. The minute you attach the shed to the gaff, or confuse the concept of a shed with the concept of a conservatory, you're doing yourself over. You're never, ever going to get spiritual enlightenment in a lean-to built onto the side of the house. That's like going to find yourself in Thailand, and staying at the airport. You need to make that pilgrimage to the bottom of the garden. Whether you're walking down a muddy track or crunching along a perfect gravel path, you have to get out of the house. Breathe in the fresh air. Then pull open the door, grapple for the light switch, fire up the heaters and turn on the kettle.

After that, it's up to you, man. Once you're inside the four walls of your shed, you can do whatever you like. You're the king in here. Exhale, as the mindfulness lot would say.

As one of the leading experts in the field of 'Shedology', with an honorary degree in the subject from the U of S, I'm lucky enough to have four sheds and I often find myself in the role of shed agony uncle to potential shed builders.

The first thing that usually comes up is, let's be honest, the cashola situation. Here's the bad news: you've got to be thinking in the two-to-seven grand region. Spending five hundred quid at B&Q is fine if you literally want somewhere to store junk that you attach no value to, but for that money you're just going to have some damp, horrible structure you're never going to want to spend any time in, and you'd be better off using the cash to hire a skip because the stuff you put in it will be ruined anyway.

If you want a den, a workspace, a private place where you can truly reconnect with what's actually important in this life, where you can focus on your needs rather than your wants, nurture your soul and incubate your creativity, then you are going to have to be open to adding another zero on the end.

My first shed as an adult cost me five grand. I built it with my mate Guy. It's four metres square, it's got carpet on the floor, two workbenches, shelves for my collection of petrol cans and a tea and coffee making area.

It's a lot of dough, and I don't mean to minimize it, but

also, you don't want your shed built on sand. You need a solid base practically in order to have a solid base emotionally and spiritually.

The key to a proper shed is that it's a place you actually want to spend time in. That means you've got to have heat and light, so you've got to have a proper power connection, not a heavy-duty extension cord. It's also got to be dry, so you need concrete foundations, more on which later.

I strongly lobby for carpet on the floor if you want the shed to be a place where you want to hang out, whether you're working on the bike or not. It's got to be just as good a place to be a human *being* as to be a human *doing*.

So realistically, that's seven grand if you get someone to do it for you, two-to-four if you do some or all of it yourself.

Now, this is your penthouse shed, but, unfortunately, there is no middle ground – you either go all the way and pimp your crib to the max or the alternative is a miserable shed that is freezing cold, with water coming in and things getting wrecked in it.

Even if you spend the dosh, you've got to understand a shed does have what is referred to in the trade as 'a shed life', and that life probably is ten years, maybe a bit more if you do the proper weather-proofing every year which we'll get to later.

A cheap shed is a mess and you just don't want to be in it. So you park your bike in it and you leave. I want a shed where I can park the bike, and think, I'll give it a clean. I want a shed where, if someone said to me, 'Henry, sleep in here tonight,' I'd say, 'Fine. Give me a sleeping bag and I'll kip on the floor.' (That said, do try and avoid sleeping in a shed. Don't let it become a weapon at times of marital discord, as per Commandment Five. Because yes, you can sleep in the shed, but by doing that you change the whole aspect of a shed into a bedroom, and that's not going to be good for your soul.)

The point of the shed is that it is another space, but for it to be another space you must leave it, and leave your endeavour. Close the door, walk back up the garden, go into your house, return to the real world and go to bed.

Similarly, a toilet is not required in a shed. For starters, al fresco urinating is where it's at, and, number two, so to speak, a shed's not a place where you curl one. Save it for the house. I have a real problem with having a loo in a shed. You can al fresco widdle, and if you really need a more lengthy bathroom engagement, it's a good opportunity to pop in and see the wife. 'All right, love, I'll just grab a cup of tea. I'm just going to use the loo.' And then as things sort of, you know, start to emanate smell-wise, you can leave and go back to your shed. Having vacated, you can vacate.

And there would be nothing worse than somebody coming into your shed and taking a poo, right? That said, I had a double garage at my last place where I had a few bikes and cars and things and I thought it would be great just to have a bog in the middle of the shed. No walls, just put a loo in and I could just sit there and look at my collection.

If a bona fide emergency strikes you do have the opportunity, if you dig a hole, to have a poo with a view. That's pretty spiritual, as long as you're using biodegradable bog paper and you fill the hole in afterwards.

The point is, the shed is a refuge from the complexities of house life. Shed life is about the simple way of life. We're looking to avoid the accoutrements of the house, such as toilets. That's what shed dwelling is all about.

I do believe that a man's shed is primarily a place where he does his hobby, which is some form of manual endeavour. He may, if he is cunning, be able to turn the hobby into a job, but, assuming he is still at hobby stage, he doesn't have to be actually engaged in doing that hobby all the time, by which I mean if you want to take five days out of life to rebuild the front-end on a Triumph, that's cool, but sometimes it's sweet just to sit there, drink tea and *look* at your hobby.

I heartily recommend it. In fact, one of my sheds is just for looking at my bikes in. I've got my Chop, my Nortons, my beloved Brough Superior, a few other bikes and a fold-up fishing chair. I go down there most days, have a cup of tea and a vape, and just have a look at them. I check there's no rust creeping in (one thing I cannot abide in a shed is rust) and I just sit and commune with them.

I have to admit, I do talk to my machinery a bit. Not too much, but I like to have a word now and again. The Chopper is in here because I rode Route 66 on her and I made her a promise, as we were coming out of Chicago. I said: 'It's up to you. If you are nice to me and keep me safe all the way to Los Angeles, I will retire you to a warm carpeted garage in the UK where you don't have to do a stroke for the rest of your life. But if you mess me about, I'll sell you to some git who's going to customize you.'

She looked after me and so now she just chills. I clean her and she's on trickle charge all the time. She just sits there by my Healey and I love her. You see, I don't break my word. If I say I'm going to do something, I'll do it. And yes, that is a bit weird when you're talking about giving your word to an inanimate object like a motorcycle, but for me, spiritually, it's important. I said I'd retire her and I have.

I am doing something that means something when I am in my shed. What, polishing an oil can means something? Damn right! I'm preserving a part of history. In my own little way, I'm actually leaving a legacy. I know it sounds crazy, but if I restore a Mobylette moped, right, that counts for something. For me, the challenge of getting it going, the satisfaction of actually doing that, the thrill of actually riding something that's been in a shed for fifty years and no one's gone to it, 'You all right, mate? I'll take you aside, I like you and I'm going to get you going,' is a very real, tangible thing.

The thing that non-shed dwellers forget about loving an inanimate object is that you still get so much value from it, because a lot of the reward of love is in the putting out of it, not the getting back of it. And an inanimate object doesn't answer back. Even my dog answers back. I was stroking it on the bed this morning and it suddenly decided to ravage my hand because I had obviously stroked it when it didn't want to be stroked. So there's a solace in resto. There is a solace and there's a rejuvenation that goes on in fixing something in the shed.

The worst thing a model railway enthusiast can do is finish his model. He needs to start another one right away. It's the same with restorations. The minute you restore a bike, you've done it and, well, what next? That's why people sell their restorations, because they want to start another.

By sitting and looking at your hobby over a cup of tea in the morning, whether it's a collection of Daleks or classic Ferraris, you're getting a five-minute therapy session. A shed is a place to immerse yourself in your hobby, and that provides refuge from the insanity of the outside world. The shed is the womb. It's the place to retreat to and do what you're really supposed to be doing on this earth. There's no time limit imposed on a visit to the shed, provided you return to the house to sleep. So, your therapy session can last thirty seconds over a cup of tea one morning when the wife's on your case, or three days if you fancy getting stuck in to those wheel forks at long last.

The shed is pure escapism. It's a place that can be yours. You can design it and create an environment (it's a bit like the aforementioned model railway in that respect). And that's the key thing about shed dwelling; it's the one place where everything happens entirely on your terms. I am the president of my own shed. And it's either my way or the highway in my shed. You decide what you want to do. You decide how it's going to be but the key to success is that what goes on in the shed couldn't possibly go on in the house. For instance, I wouldn't recommend stripping a BSA Gold

Star engine in your twin Belfast sink. You're going to get divorced. So, anything that could cause a rift between you and your partner, which is legal and above board and you don't feel guilty about afterwards, must be done in the shed.

On a spiritual and mental level, I think you can't do anything criminal in a shed. Of course, you could melt down gold bullion but really, for that, you need a lock-up, not a shed, and that's why a lock-up may be a physical refuge (from the cops), but it's never going to be a place that builds up your mental reserves and fortifies your soul in the positive way that a shed does.

Spending time in a shed engaged in productive manual endeavour can completely alter a man's outlook. It can change his direction and it can change his mind.

I think it is because of what a shed implies: that you are just looking after the basic elements that make you happy, and doing without the frills and the foreign holidays. We all know, deep down, that materialism actually in the end does not make you happy. If it did, then why is Christmas the most universally feared time of year? All that spending of money, all that getting of stuff, it's like a drug. Actually, it's not like a drug. It *is* a drug. Once you've taken a little bit of it, you want a little bit more and a little bit more and a little bit more. And then, instead of owing your dealer eighty quid, you actually owe the HP company fifty grand. It's exactly the same principle: give them a nibble to get them started and soon they'll be begging for more than they can afford, or need or want.

Unless you're absolutely sure of what you want, then

wanting stuff is a worry. For instance, if you've always dreamt of owning a Willys Jeep, and you actually save up the money to buy that Willys Jeep and that Willys Jeep is as good as you thought it was going to be, then I think that kind of materialism is okay. But if, after buying a Willys Jeep, you want a T-72 tank, and then you want a Wessex helicopter with military spec, then I think you have a problem.

In a shed, you make something. It's a place where the satisfaction of creation, or creating something, or preserving something benefits your soul. Whereas materialism is the quick fix, the sugar rush in comparison to the stew. So a shed and unfettered materialism just don't go together in spiritual harmony.

A shed is somewhere where you find out about yourself while doing the work of creating the thing that you wanted materialistically, by which I mean you can go and buy a Willys Jeep for twenty grand right now, but I saw one this morning for seven and a half that needs finishing – well, I say finishing, but you know it needs a year's work on it. But if you bought that seven and a half grand Willys and then you actually learnt, if you didn't know, how to restore it (it's a very basic vehicle so you will get there in the end) and made mistakes along the way, and got humbled by it, and hit your thumb with a hammer and drank millions of cups of tea and got your mates round to help you get the wheel off – well, isn't that so much more enthralling and spiritually uplifting and rewarding than going to buy a Willys for twenty grand this afternoon like it is an Xbox in Argos?

And the real beauty of it is that you may think you're just restoring a Jeep, but in fact you are being submerged in the life-changing magic of sheds, and the life-changing magic of sheds will happen to you whether or not you wanted it, or expected it, or planned for it, or thought you didn't need it in the first place.

2:
Building Your Utopia

There was a time when a man would say, 'I want to build a shed,' and we would all have known exactly what he wanted to do. A shed was a load of shiplap or plywood slapped together with a floor of earth, and hey presto, you've created a shed from some detritus that's knocking around. The junkyard challenge, basically.

Well, those days are well over. My advice is to buy an off the peg shed that is pre-fabricated in some way, but can be customized too. You can order it online but it's probably a good idea to go into a shed showroom and have a look round a few if this is your first rodeo. You can either get self-assembly or you can get a couple of lovely local lads who come round and do it for you as part of the price.

If you get onto these people who are purveyors of sheds, they will these days offer you a whole load of options: do you want a storage space, do you want a garage, do you want a log cabin, do you want a home office, do you want a shepherd's hut with wheels to stop the rats getting in?

If you are building a new shed you should resist the temptation to build a kind of lean-to off the side of it to store wood under. It's very tempting, but it will damage the sense of a self-contained utopia if you start attaching other things onto it like wood shelters and stuff. The more you attach, the more it becomes like a favela. You're better to use your shed for your first project: building a little wood shelter.

I digress (a frequent problem with shed chat); the point is, it's worth having a think about what you might actually want to do in your shed because the key to happy shed dwelling is proper planning. You need to decide, firstly, what size shed you actually want and what it's going to be there for. What I want for a shed is for it to fulfil three basic functions, the triumvirate of shed functionality as I like to think of it: a place to sit, a place to fettle and a place to stash. A shed has to fit its purpose.

Let's say you're a biker, and you want to restore things, and the things you really dream of restoring are Triumph Bonneville motorcycles. Well, immediately then, when you're constructing your shed, you don't need double doors, do you? You just need a single door to get the bikes in. And that actually means an awful lot in terms of cash and expense and draught and storage, wall space and . . . well, everything.

Most of my sheds are only bike accessible, but loads of people restore cars in sheds, which means they've got to have double doors (and in fact I'm just finishing a big shed further down the way with a car lift in it which is purpose-built for that exact practice of restoring cars and getting things on a ramp). But, if you're not going to restore a car, your shed has more flexibility.

With bikes, even if the shed is small, you can still have two or three on the go at any one time if you fancy it. You don't have to have big double doors, you don't have to have the height to get a car on a ramp. So, your shed innately can be an awful lot smaller if you're doing motorcycles, stationary engines, petrol pumps, all that kind of stuff.

But it's something that you should plan or have a think about. Yes, of course you need to future-proof stuff, but at the same time if you're a dyed in the wool biker, you really don't need height to a shed, yeah? If you're going to restore cars or boats or something like that, then you need a lot more space, you need a lot more height and you need to think about where everything is going to go, because moving that stuff around is going to be hard work. You need the machinery, like engine lifts and all that kind of stuff, everything's bigger if you're dealing with cars, so, consequently they're much less movable. The flexibility of how your shed's laid out can mean your choices are some-what narrowed because of the amount and the size of the equipment that you need to use. If you're really going to get involved in the chassis and getting underneath the motor and that kind of stuff you need height, and you need room around the doors so the doors can open. So, all in all, if you're going to do cars, you need a big shed. I mean you're verging on a warehouse.

People do have huge bits of equipment (hello, lorry fans) that they're restoring and it's absolutely vital to get your shed right for what you want.

A concrete pad on which your shed will stand is pivotally important, but it's the element that people most often forget or ignore when they are working out the cost of building a shed. The concrete slab on which your shed stands should not be its actual floor. (Although a garage is going to have a concrete floor, people just accept that, but here's a top tip: concrete dust is a nightmare, so I'd suggest you go to an auto jumble and buy a stack of carpet tiles. I'll get a batch of five hundred for eighty quid and then I'll lay them myself on any concrete floor.)

But let's talk about the slab: you will need that concrete pad to stand your shed on. You can try all the alternatives, such as laying a brick base, raising it up on blocks, or even building it on saddle stones so it's two feet in the air but, in the end, without a concrete pad, for it to sit on, it's not actually going to work because it is going to let water ingress and it's not going to be solid when a storm comes.

The only alternative is a kind of plastic grid system that you lay on flat ground, and you fill it with gravel, etc. and then build the shed on that. That can be doable, and it's more ecologically friendly, because you're not creating massive great concrete slabs, so I do use that sometimes as well. But the concrete base, if you're planning on building the quintessential shed, is probably where it's at.

I'd say you ideally want to make your shed five metres by three metres – that for me is perfect if you're not having a car in there. If you're having a car, then it's five metres by four and a half metres, double doors and all that kind of stuff. You can go smaller but the minimum you can get away with really is three metres by three metres.

Anyway, to put that concrete base in, a builder is going to charge you around two grand. And people overlook that. Now, if you're of a DIY disposition, and you have got the time, great. You can shave that cost off, lay your own hardcore and put concrete over the top. I don't have the time or skillset to do that so, Paul, my builder, who's a legend, comes in and he lays the base. And he makes sure it's just got a very slight angle on it so rainwater will run off, because what you really don't want is the water actually lying on the concrete slab and then running under the shed.

Also, prior to you or your builder pouring that slab, you need to think about what kind of electrics you're going to want because you may want electricity to come up through the concrete, through the floor of the shed in some way. Personally, I don't do it like that. I just have it coming in as a feed through the wall to the junction box.

Also, you need to decide where you want the sun to be. Most shed dwellers tend to put windows on only one side of the shed because there's no point a lot of the time in having windows, because sheds don't generally have views (a subject we will discuss in more detail later), and because they use up valuable shelf, storage and workbench space. Obviously, it's tempting to say the windows should face south. But, actually, be aware that as the sun comes in through south-facing windows (or from skylights) it will a) cook you in summer and b) fade items that you have left there and forgotten about. Fading is something you really need to be aware of. So, if you've got a beautiful BSA Bantam and you park it in the shed is by the south-facing window, well, over time, the sun will fade the colour, so just beware.

Now obviously, one part of the shed has got to be north facing. And, with that north-facing side being colder, you might think you don't want the windows to be north facing, unless steady light is really important to you because you are going to be painting in there or doing stop-motion movies on your iPad.

So try and think about how the sun is going to interact with your shed and what your priorities are before you start pouring that slab. Think about the outside as well, because maybe you're going to want to sit outside in the evening in the summer with the doors of your shed open while you clean something or enjoy your garden, in which case, face the doors west. But if you're a morning person, it might be smarter to have your main outside area facing east. Whatever, just remember the location of the shed is critical and there is a feng shui element like in any room.

But the joy of a shed is that instead of walking into a room and thinking 'This is how I have got to change it,' with a shed you are starting from scratch. You not only get to decide how big and what shape this new room is, but you get to decide exactly where that room is going to be located. You're not pandering to 'Well, it's just off the kitchen.' You have complete control. It's your own room, and it can be wherever you want it to be.

Some people like to have a shed with a view, but I don't think it's necessary for a shed to have a view. I'm not entirely crazy about houses with a view because views mean that you're exposed to the wind. Now, in a house, maybe you will want a view and accept the commensurate exposure to the wind, because you can stay inside and keep the windows closed ten months of the year, but wind and a shed do not go together. You just don't feel content in a gale in a shed. The wind wrecks your equilibrium, because you do feel that at any moment your shed roof's going to come off. I've been in sheds with wonderful views where you can't open the door because of the wind. If you open the door of a shed in a gale and you've got a view, it means that basically the chances are the door's going to get ripped off.

That brings us onto another point, which is that you need a sturdy retaining hook and eye system, so that when you want to open the door, you can secure the door open. If you don't do that, it's spiritually, mentally and physically concerning, because the door is flapping in the wind and squeeking. And if the door comes off your shed, well, your internals are exposed to the elements and to other people. So, you need to secure it with a hook and eye system and you also need, I think, to make sure that the shed is in a secluded position.

Why would you want a view anyway? If you're doing what you should be doing in a shed you'll be concentrating on whatever it may be. Sheds are internal situations. The energy is focused inwards. The other thing to remember about a view is they go both ways – and you don't want anyone to know you've got a shed really, apart from people you invite.

Just because you don't want a view, is not to say that your shed shouldn't be a thing of beauty, and a bit of flora can help that cause massively. It seems to me that a lot of shed dwellers combine their love of sheds with a development of a love for gardening. A good way to start off is with said flora attached to your shed, in the form of hanging baskets and window boxes. Hanging baskets are another good argument for your shed to be shielded from the wind because otherwise your herbaceous hanger could actually end up knocking you out on a windy day.

But, assuming the risk of physical danger can be precluded, do try a couple of hanging baskets. They give me a real sense of delight, they attract the bees and butterflies, which makes me feel good, and they also show the seasons changing as well, which I enjoy. I now actually go one stage further and I like having a tiny garden by a shed if at all possible, and I am not averse to some small windowsill plants within the shed as well. It's all about nourishing the soul.

Another consideration in your shed build is the matter of insulation. Cashflow-wise, you can halve the price, sometimes, of your pre-packed, self-assembly shed, if you don't ask for insulation. If they do try and sell it to you, resist. I don't have insulation in any of my sheds. None. There's quite a few reasons for that being my preference, but mainly it is because with insulation comes issues.

The main issue, indeed the fundamental truth that arises at every twist and turn of shed life, is that a shed is not a house. If a shed is made as airtight as a house, but without the fancy ventilation and heat recovery systems that modern airtight houses have, then it doesn't allow things to breathe and you can have a majorly negative situation with vapour build-up. The thing is, when you breathe and talk you expel water vapour, and if there isn't even just a tiny, wiggly little bit of airflow, then that water vapour can't go anywhere. It gets trapped and you get condensation and mould.

Secondly, what do you actually want insulation for? To retain heat. Well, a much better use of your cash is to get thicker walls because if you get the thickness of the walls right, then, I humbly suggest, you will actually only need minimal heat. Thicker walls are good for the general solidity of the shed. They also have the advantage of keeping the heat out in the summer and stopping it becoming an oven. The reality is you will not notice a difference between insulated and non-insulated sheds, as regards their retention of heat, so, personally, I don't believe it's worth spending the money. Indeed, excessive heat can be as much of a problem as cold.

But, yes, for four months of the year it's going to be cold. So get a little oil-filled heater, maybe 0.5W, plug it in every November and turn it off in March. That will cost you around twenty quid a month, and everything in the shed will stay lovely and dry. I do suggest you also have a blow heater for the instant hit when you walk in, just to get it up to a pleasant temperature quickly. That is the way forward.

It's vital to remember that the absolute killer in a shed is damp. I know I'm not saving the planet by leaving a heater on, but I am saving my shed, and given that my most beloved things are in my sheds, I just can't risk condensation or dampness.

Condensation, incidentally, is another reason I would

promote the idea of having a wooden building, because in a steel frame building there are major issues with condensation. Hot air rises and it evaporates on the cold steel roof which creates condensation that drips down on whatever you've got in there. Very nasty.

I do think wood is really the only way to go when you're building a shed. Quite apart from the issue with the condensation, there's an emotional issue. A steel shed just feels like a warehouse or a storage unit. Wood is a much more engaging material to use. You can feel it, you can smell it. It's just . . . it's just lovely.

Now, when they ask you about the thickness of the walls, I would try, if possible, to go no thinner than 45mm thick for the wood that the shed is created out of. This thickness gives a certain rigidity and a retention of heat. If you go for 25mm or something like that, the shed innately is more flexible, you feel that it's less solid and less of a building to be safe in and you're worried about the elements, etc. It's just the thicker the walls, the safer you feel. It gives your shed a bit of cred.

But sheds move. The walls of them, I mean. They are made of spruce, it's usually green, it hasn't seasoned and it's going to season when it's made up as a shed in situ, and with that it shrinks, it cracks, it moves, whatever. And you need to be aware of that, and not get on to the shed people and go, 'It's moved,' because they will just say: 'Well, it's wood, what do you expect?' Insulation can make the consequences of the movement issue worse because the insulation is totally synthetic and doesn't move with the wood.

Where I do believe it's worth spending extra money is on the roof. Normally sheds are supplied with a basic felt over a wooden roof, but I always go one stage further and have shingle asphalt tiles. Shingle keeps the shed warm in winter and cool in summer, but it also makes sure the roof really is 200 per cent waterproof. And a great roof on a shed means you can forgive a few other cut corners.

Another very practical thing to think about when you are considering the location of your shed and pouring a slab, is to figure out about power. If you're a million miles away from the power to your house, it's going to cost you a bit more money to get it hooked up. And you want to be on the mains because you've got to run power points, you've got to run lights, you've got to run the heat, and power tools. Even as a non-electrician, I can definitively say it's downright dangerous running an extension lead down there and you really don't want your energy supply cutting out at 6pm on a wet Wednesday in November when the kids are driving you crazy and you really need to get out to the shed and have a cup of tea.

Unless you are really doing some specialist stuff in your shed, you should just be able to use regular 13 amp plug sockets. But again, try and think here about what power points you want. I've made the mistake over the years of putting power points at ground level, same as in a house, or just six inches above the ground. Actually, in a shed, the power points need to be above the workbench. I actually tend to leave the power points till the very end. I get the workbench in, and then think where I need the plugs. I'm never in a rush to finish the shed. I like to enjoy the process of actually creating my own world.

A good tip for lighting (I'm actually just doing it now with a big shed that I'm refurbishing) is to have the plug sockets on two separate circuits, and then on one of those circuits, let's call it circuit B, have a master switch by the door. Then you can plug all your lamps, all your illuminated signs, all your anglepoise lamps, your garage signs, all that stuff into circuit B sockets, which look different to circuit A sockets, (maybe they are bronze or chrome or whatever) and they all go on and off with one click of a switch at the front door. Then your other circuit, circuit A, that's like a normal plug circuit, you just switch them on and off at the socket, and they are for your trickle chargers or your computers or your background heater – stuff that you just leave on or switch off at the wall in the normal way.

It makes all the difference on a cold dark night, let me tell you, to be able to instantly transform your shed into a warm and welcoming womb-like space. And when you leave, it's handy too, otherwise it takes me half an hour to switch off all the lamps and knackers my back. Without power you have no heat, and without heat, in my humble opinion, you don't really have what I mean when I talk about a shed. I just don't understand people who don't keep their sheds warm.

Heat is vital because a shed really comes into its own in the winter months. In the summer, you won't really be there that much as a biker, because you are out on the road. Sheds are September to March affairs. Get it heated, get the kettle on, avoid the family at all costs and you can start to be at peace. I mean, cheap heating is one of the major perks of modern life, isn't it? If you ain't going to heat the shed, you might as well just go and sit under a tree to get away from the wife.

The fundamental problem with no heating is that you don't want to be there. Why do you want to be anywhere that is freezing cold? I tell you, if I inherited a freezing cold castle in Scotland I'd sell it and turn it into an NCP car park (multi-storey) and move into a lovely warm cosy cottage down the road.

You can buy a heater for twenty quid but some people prefer to build another shed to house a biomass boiler. Well, I say shed, but really it's a barn you'll be needing. One mate of mine has got a shed with a biomass boiler in it, this gigantic edifice at the end of his garden that is bigger than his house. 'It's great,' he says, 'I heat my house and the water, and I put power back on the national grid.' 'What?' I say. 'Why are you making electricity for other people? They have power stations for that, mate.'

As with insulation, I don't think it's worth spending money on frost-proofing. In fact, I'll go further: frost-proofing your shed, unless you have some specific need to do so, is the most ridiculous concept in the world. All you need is a twenty quid heater. You get one, you switch it on and you leave it on, and not only is your shed now frost-free, it's also damp-free. Dampness, not coldness, is the thing that will kill your shed in the long run and that's why you need a little heater on at all times just to take the edge off. I actually keep a heater on a thermostat plugged in during the summer, just in case you get one of those unexpectedly frosty nights. I reckon it adds pennies to my summer electricity bill, a price well worth paying. There's no sense going to town with major construction when you can plug in a heater from Tesco.

Of course, if you are really serious about tackling damp, the other thing that's really useful in a shed is a dehumidifier. Now, these can be quite expensive, like 200 quid upwards, but you have to remember how absolutely lethal damp is in a shed-like environment. No one wants you to have rusty nuts, least of all your wife.

Moisture is the shed's biggest killer, but it's important to get the right size dehumidifier, because if you're not careful, they can dry everything out and, over time, all your rubber hosing and that kind of stuff will start to perish because it's so dry and cracked. So, you need to get the compromise right and that takes a bit of trial and error to be honest, but a good starting point is to establish the volume of your shed and buy something of an appropriate size. Once you've got it, it'll last you a good while; and if all your nuts rust, it'll cost you way more than 200 quid to put right.

Sheds are a utopia of peace and contentment, even if it's next to a road and you can hear the ambulances blaring down the A1. (An exposed shed by the road, where someone with a drop-side pick-up can easily see it, is not to be recommended, although I do quite like a little bit of intermittent road noise to remind me I'm alive.) But even if you can hear the emergency services and the neighbours screaming at each other, in the shed, if it's warm and cosy, you feel safe and secure. That's what shedding is all about.

Taking the plunge into shed dwelling is metaphorically about building your world, but if you are lucky enough to have the time, the skills and a few generous mates to help you, then actually physically building your own shed is one of the best ways you can spend two weeks of your life. I know what I'm talking about because I've done it a few times now. You can definitely bring the cost right down to two grand, especially if you can do the concrete base yourself and have some experience in this area. I know guys who have gone all out and constructed their sheds from scratch but I really wouldn't advise that unless you have some special reason to do so, because it is so easy to buy a really decent flat-pack shed.

If you build it yourself, that is what therapy is all about. Not only are you going to find spiritual contentment inside the four walls of your shed when it's done, the life-changing magic of sheds will be starting to exert its mysterious power on you long before you fix your first brake pad during that actual building process.

Don't worry too much if you've never done it before. Everyone has to do something for the first time, and the important thing is just to get stuck in. But, at the same time, be ready to call in the professionals if things start going awry or you get overwhelmed by it. Obviously, the best thing is to have a mate who has maybe done a bit of building who will help out, but if things are really going tits up, you know what? There's no shame in looking up a local builder on the Internet and asking him to come and finish it for you.

That's actually the core of shed dwelling, right there. It's a place where it's okay to make mistakes and it's okay to ask for help to learn how to fix those mistakes, something I'm going to be ranting on about a bit later. Maybe, when you finish it you'll think, 'I really should have done this bit a different way,' but that's okay, man. That's how we learn, that's how we enrich our lives in sheds.

I'm guessing, if you're set on a shed, you're probably at least forty-something and you're starting off on that next chapter of life, because, let's face it, the shed chapters are the second half of the book of life, aren't they? There are not many twenty-year-olds going, 'I want to get a shed!' But if you're actually going to learn something over the age of forty, and physically go and do it, it's got to be good, hasn't it? And as mentioned above, if you finish it and there's a blooming great hole in it, you can get on to Bob the Builder and say, 'Bob, I built a shed and actually I can see planes going overhead. Can you help me out?' And he'll probably say, 'Of course mate, I'll come over tomorrow and take a look,' and he'll sort it out for you or show you how to sort it out yourself. People like sharing their skills. For all the risk of it going wrong, do it, because there's something massively energizing and satisfying about thinking, 'I've never actually built anything before, but I'm going to look up how to pour a concrete slab.'

It's about wiring up parts of your brain you have either never used or not used for a very long time. You hear a lot, don't you, about how important it is to keep learning all your life and blah, blah, blah and all of that, but very few of us actually do it. Very few adults, with the exception of shed dwellers, ever actually try and do something that we don't already know how to do.

I had that experience the other day taking out fence posts. I went on YouTube and looked it up. They said drill holes through the post, put a bolt through it and then lever the bolt with a jack. And it'll pull fence posts out of a concrete pad. I thought, 'That's got to be a load of rubbish,' but I went and got an old jack and tried it and it works brilliantly. Now, what works even better is my mate Matt with his telehandler, but that costs and there's no joy in it. I mean, there is joy in the end result, but being a shed dweller is about finding joy in doing this stuff. It's about doing something you have never done before and seeing how you get on.

But building a shed is not something to do on your own. You've got to get a mate to help you. You can't construct a shed on your own for practical reasons (obviously sometimes the purlins and things are just a bit too long and you can't hold them up) but also emotional reasons: the actual building of a shed is like conceiving a child. You need a partner in crime to go, 'Hey, Lawrence, does that look all right, is that straight or what?' And you need someone to share in the fulfilment of achieving shed glory. And you need that to be shared with someone, with a friend. It won't be shared with your wife. She's not interested. Don't ask her. She may feign interest but fake interest in a shed is worse than no interest at all.

3:
Various Non-alternatives to Sheds, and Why They Are a Bad Idea

A shed is the best. It has no equal. But I suppose I should at least acknowledge that some alternative structures exist, not that any sane individual should consider them.

First up, shepherd's huts. I think part of the reason all these bean eaters nowadays like shepherd's huts is a planning thing. If the council come round you can just wheel it into the barn. And probably that really is the only time you will ever wheel it anywhere. But why would you want to move it? I mean, what would you want to do that for? Just put it in the best place and leave it there. And in that case, why not be the master of your own destiny and build a shed? Also, you can't get a motorbike, or anything heavy, into a shepherd's hut. If you did get it in, it would drop through the floor.

Shepherd's huts are decorative items really, and they can look lovely, but I think the idea of them is better than the reality, especially when you're on the 8:42 into Euston with your *Country Living* magazine. So I don't go a bundle on shepherd's huts. I'd prefer a treehouse. And the last time I stayed in a treehouse, I did an epic poo and blocked up the composting bog.

While we are on the subject of non-alternatives to sheds, let me just say: you don't want to 'contain' a man. What I mean is that while I've slept in containers that have been converted into very nice hotels, I'd never recommend one as a shed. The problems are manifold, but firstly: if you are really going to create somewhere that you actually want to go to, then a container is not the place, unless you spend a lot of money on it. Containers predominantly are for storage, not for human endeavour or human existence. Secondly, your place looks like a dump yard with a container in it. Containers aren't aesthetically pleasing to me, or to anyone in their right mind. They just look like some lorry's just dropped it off from the docks and forgotten about it. 'When's he coming again to remove it?' is the only question to ask when confronted with a container in a man's garden. I just don't like them.

The only sensible reason for people to bring containers into their world is to actually store valuable stuff in because they are secure, but honestly, a shed is still a better choice because containers innately are damp because they're metal. I've never actually found anything that I really wanted to take home in a container. They're full of detritus normally, and stuff that is slowly composting or rusting away. If you leave something in a container long enough, the condensation is going to wreck it. You can line them, okay, so then they are dry – but why do that when actually you might as well use the money to build another shed?

Containers are terrible but yurts are truly absurd. They're a total avocado-eating proposition. Honestly, man. I mean you buy a yurt, next thing you know you'll be plaiting your pubes. I can't see the point of a yurt unless it's for renting out to pube-plaiters, who turn up in Volkswagen camper vans, to make money. In which case; fine, we all gotta live, but count me out, I really don't want those people in my garden. I mean, they're going to sit down and meditate, aren't they? They're going to get all cross-legged about it, with the yoga, the marinated bean sprouts and the live cultures and I mean that's just not shedding. That's a whole different ballgame.

A more viable alternative to building a new shed is repurposing an old one. But repurposing an existing shed is a gamble. Let's just say you buy yourself a house, and there's a shed in the garden, right? So, you go into that shed, and there's water coming in, but it's a cool shed and you love it so you decide to fix it. Now the reality is it's probably going to cost you more to repurpose that shed to how you want it than taking it down and putting a new one up. I'm going through that process right now with a twelve-metre by eight-metre shed. I'm only doing it out of love. Well, love and planning. Existing structure and all that. But, generally, if the shed is below 2.5m high, you don't need planning, which is pretty sensible really because if it's low enough that no one's going to notice it, then, fire away. If I put a skyscraper up, on the other hand, I'm asking for trouble.

Usually, I wouldn't bother repurposing a shed, but the

one I'm doing now is a particularly lovely shed and Paul, our builder, totally sorted it out. Of course, by the time he had lined it out, poured a concrete floor, reinforced the roof, cut a bloody great hole in the wall, installed double doors, put a hundred plug points in and replaced the joists it would have been cheaper to build a new shed. The fiscal advantage of reconditioning an old shed versus building a new one is none, zero, but I'm into old stuff, so I feel it's incumbent on me to retain shed heritage when I find it, and this was a cracker.

I think sometimes you see a shed that speaks to you and asks you to save it and that was the case here. It had been there forever and now, thanks to me (well, okay, thanks to Paul) it'll be here forever again. I like the idea of putting our heritage into something with heritage, rather than just craning in a brand new steel frame shed overnight. That shed is everything to me. It's a classic shed, classic construction, a bit of shiplap, a decent roof and away you go.

Opposite it, however, there is an old shed that has to come down because it's a classic rubbish shed. It's open fronted, which means there is no point in building that shed because it actually doesn't encapsulate the items that you want to put in it. That is the worst shed you can possibly have. It's ugly. You can't sit in it. You can't shut the doors on it. And it's got no smell.

The smell of a shed is critical. It's the first thing that got me into shed dwelling. If you've got an open bay, there's no smell because it's all dissipating into the ether. Now, I've actually got a 135 Massey Ferguson parked in there and not only is that aesthetically a lovely thing, and totally functional, but it also smells of lovely old diesel. So not only is she getting well cold, but also there's no smell, right?

That musty, oily smell of the shed takes me back to one of my first great experiences in a wooden structure. When I was a kid, I went up the road to the village hall that was disused. It was a shed, a massive green shed, about the size of a small house. And I broke in – well, I just went through the window that was already broken – and there was a full-size billiard table in there, and I played billiards with two balls, not three, and no cue.

The smell of that shed will always be with me. And when I go into other sheds, it's that musty smell that does it for me. That smell tells me I am in a safe place, in the womb, in my utopia. From my shed I can hear the guns on Salisbury Plain and I can hear the emergency services going past, but they can't get to me. There's no hassle there. There's no politicians and no bullshit, and if I don't like you, you can't come in. I'm just doing my thing, you know. And that is the joy of it.

And an open fronted shed can never deliver that. It's just a cold catcher. A rain catcher.

So, yes, smell and watertightness are vital components but aesthetically, it's got to look lovely too.

If you're really splashing out on your shed, and it's big enough, a great thing to have is what they used to call a 'dirty room', and it ain't what you're thinking, mister. A dirty room is like where the messy work happens so you have a pillar drill, band saws, bench sanders, grinders and all that kind of stuff in there. It's a place where you can make a mess, spill oil and get dust everywhere and it doesn't matter. Dirty rooms are great for spraying paint as well, which is a really important part of any restoration. It's just very helpful to be able to separate the shed to have an area where you can do all that stuff and an area which is clean and pristine, because there are moments when you need both at the same time. Just having the facility to keep the dirty work away from the main shed changes your shed life completely.

4:
Break and Enter
My Shed at Your
Own Risk

Shed security is a troublesome issue, but, at the end of the day, you have to remember that locks only keep out honest men. Putting twenty-seven padlocks on the door of your shed, like my mate Angus does, is not only totally pointless and really annoying (trust me, when it's cold and wet, the last thing you want to be doing is messing around with a complex series of interconnected and frozen locks), it's actually going to make things worse from a security point of view. The problem is that if some dodgy geezer who is walking by sees those locks, it doesn't put him off. Not in the slightest. Actually, he is going to think, 'Hey, there must be something worth stealing in there.'

This leads inevitably on to a further problem which is that thieves, by and large, are not totally committed to the convention of only using doors to enter premises. You locked the door? He is going to break the window and come on in anyway. And what's he going to find when he gets in there? A kettle, a La-Z-boy, some woodwork tools, an old vape and your treasured collection of Bovril jars. Hardly the haul of a lifetime, so off he scoots empty-handed to go and do something sensible like some online credit card crime, and now you've got a window to replace and a load of glass to clean up.

Of course you can put bars on the window, but, er, newsflash – it's a shed. Your average criminally minded fifteen-year-old (which is what most of these little toe-rags are) can kick a hole in the wall no problem. Put bars on the window and you'll really be getting them interested. They might even get a saw.

Alarms are useless, unless you are actually looking for a device to wake you up at 3am every time there is a storm. And if by some miracle someone has actually broken in when the alarm goes off, do you think civically minded citizens are going to come sprinting to your aid to perform a citizen's arrest? No mate, they're going to be staying well clear.

The big, motion-activated floodlights some nervous shed dwellers install are no use either. Of course, if you want to have a security crisis every time a fox walks through the garden, be my guest.

Some shed owners (like some car owners) actually take the view that it's better to just leave the shed unlocked all the time, because at least that way you don't have the broken window to get fixed, but I can't quite bring myself to do that, not least because I don't want to get back to my shed (or car) and find a farting drunk guy who got lost on the way home snoring away, fast asleep in it. So a single lock is, I think, a good idea, just to keep out the opportunists (and the inebriated). It's a way to send a message to the world that it's your shed and they are not bloody welcome.

Now, of course, it's a bit different if you've got your Spyder or your Harley parked up in there, and I do keep all my really valuable bikes, my pension fund as I like to think of them, under serious lock and key. The valuable stuff is kept in what are basically windowless bunkers built out of metal or brick. They're still clean and warm, with carpet on the floor, and a chair, because I do actually like to go and hang out there for maybe fifteen to twenty minutes every day, as I've already mentioned. I have a cup of tea and a vape, and I sit there with my bikes, have a look at them, have a little chat, check everything's pukka, then I clear off and lock up after me.

One thing I am interested in is fogging. I saw it on *Crimewatch* when some bad dude was trying to rob a jeweller's. The guy gets in, right, and the alarm goes off to summon the pigs and all that, but this fog machine goes off, and you can't see anything. It's totally all encompassing. He just can't see; he can't see the end of his nose. So, he's stopped in his tracks, and if he's going to wait around for it to clear, we'll be on him. It's either that or a shotgun on a piece of string that opens up and blows the dude away which, if there were no laws, I'd do. My motto is: any person who breaks into a shed, they should really be dead.

I mean, the suite of security options is infinite, so it all depends on what you've got in there and what you want. But I tell you what's great security: make sure no one can see into the shed. So, buy yourself some £9.99 blinds, wind them down at night, lock the door and toddle off back to the house.

Shed security is important because in the event of a fire, once the family was okay and the dog was okay, I'd definitely try and save the shed before the house, and not just because the shed's made of wood so it might burn a bit quicker. The thing is that, for me, my most valuable items, spiritually and financially, are in the shed. I've got to be honest: I would rather save my Kawasaki Z1 than a picture my parents had above the mantelpiece. Because I'm really not interested in that picture but if I lose my Z1? Oh my God, I mean, the time I spent rebuilding that engine! I'm never going to get something as good as that on insurance. I'd have to safeguard my restored petrol pumps and tin signs. I'd lob them out onto the lawn as quickly as possible, put them in the pond briefly, if necessary. It's about priorities, man.

You could just be your own security, of course. Guard your domain overnight. The wife would probably be happier if you were in there till morning anyway. But you gotta obey the law, I'm not condoning any vigilante action on would-be burglars. You could arm yourself with a catapult I suppose but don't go all Dirty Harry. I mean, I was in a shed about a year ago and the guy had a howitzer in there. An artillery weapon. A massive great gun, on wheels, an artillery piece that lobs a shell twenty miles. And I said to the geezer, 'Where did you get that?' He goes, 'Oh, I picked it up from a dealer, I quite liked it.' Quite liked it! That's lucky – it takes up the whole of his shed. I said, 'Is it . . . I mean does it work?' He goes, 'Of course not. It's been deactivated.' I go,

'What does that mean?' 'Oh, well they poured some liquid metal down the barrel and that, or whatever.' I said, 'Oh. It's a shame isn't it, it doesn't work?' He goes, 'Well, with a bit of engineering here, we could get it going, I would think.' I thought, 'This guy could wheel out that howitzer, put a shell in it and lob a small one into Cleethorpes.'

There was another guy I met with a 25-pound artillery gun of the type that my father used to operate. And I go, 'Is that deactivated?' He goes, 'I'm not sure.' Which basically means 'No'.

The Americans are particularly obsessed with weaponry. I mean, if you looked at the arsenal residing in the sheds of America, you'd find enough hardware that's operating and working, you know, to invade Canada.

I mean, the things that are in sheds never cease to amaze me. I walked into one the other day and there's a Saladin armoured car there. Fully operational, with periscopes, bullet-proof glass, the whole nine yards, yeah? 'You wouldn't be wanting a Saladin armoured car, would you, Henry?' the bloke said. 'Well, not really. I don't quite know what I'd do with it.' 'Well, if you're interested, or know someone else, that'll be six grand.' 'Really? Only six grand? Well, maybe . . .'

5:
Feng Shui for Sheds

The first thing that you have to do, once you have got the shed up, is paint it inside (with paint) and out (with wood preserver). Now, the wood preserver is essential – even if they say it's treated, stick another coat on. It goes on quick but it's quite smelly, so just do that right away and feel happy in the knowledge that you just extended the life of your shed by a few years, and if you redo it every few years it will probably outlive the standard shed life expectations.

One thing I have got into recently is that there are different coloured sheds, right, for different parts of the country. So, in Hertfordshire, what they do with their sheds and barns is they paint them matt black and they look mint, so, I'm painting all our sheds matt black at the moment.

People always forget, or try and ignore, the issue of painting the inside of their shed. It's a very important stage, because the painting of the shed is where you deliver your personal touch to your world, but I've got to be honest, it's also a very laborious task because there's just so much surface area, and you've got to apply a couple of coats at least. It's going to take you a week to do it – or it's going to take someone else a week to do it and you're going to have to pay them for it. My mate Guy and I put up the first couple of sheds and painted them ourselves and there is a real magic in building and painting your own shed (mind you, there's also a certain magic in me not having to raise a finger; but it's expensive magic).

What you need to do is get the four walls that you're surrounded by to be something that you love, and for me, that is pastel colours. like Cotswold green, or baby blue. I for one am in touch with my feminine side when it comes to painting pastel colours. So, the colour of your shed, the interior of it is really interesting. You can tell a lot about a person by the colour they choose, and I don't mean in a hippy 'colour therapy' way. What I mean is that if someone paints their shed in very bright white colours, for example, they'll have an engineering bias, and they'll want to have bright lights so they can see what they're doing.

After you've done the paint job, it's the really fun and creative bit, which is decorating and accessorizing your shed. I love this phase of the shed adventure. I put up all the shelving, mess around with the lighting and put my vintage petrol cans out, because I've got to make the place work for me aesthetically, and slowly but surely it turns into my sacred utopia.

I was dropping off a gearbox to a mate of mine the other day and we go into his shed, and there are three racks of gleaming 1980s race bikes in there. Now, these are my favourite kinds of bikes of all time, it was immaculate, the workbench was there and all the bits were in place, but I felt spiritually bereft as we looked at them. I was thinking about this afterwards, what was it that was wrong about the place? And then I realized that it was because there was nowhere to sit down, and every shed has to have a few battered deckchairs or a scruffy old sofa, a place where you can take the weight off your feet, and maybe hang out with your mates if you and they are so inclined, a place where you can just chill.

As mentioned earlier, I think that the perfect shed has three areas: sit, store and fettle. First, you do need a place to sit down with your mates and have a cup of tea (and that may be just one little sofa or a couple of stools); then you've got a tinkering area, where you've got a little lathe, perhaps, or your workbench; and then you've got a collecting area, the area where you put your bikes, or your car that you love, or your stationary engine that you love, or whatever it is. And if you've got a shed that can incorporate all those three things, then I think you've got the ultimate shed.

Lighting is critical. For me, I want soft light, you know, practical lamps with those Edison bulbs in to give that kind of old heritage look, although I do have strip lighting that I can switch on when I'm working on a machine or I want to sort out the electrics on a motorbike or work with Sammy to rebuild something, or whatever it is.

We're old fellas with dodgy eyes, so we need really good light. The worst thing possible is to have bad light in a shed if you're going to work in it. So, the perfect thing is to have two forms of lighting. Chilled lights that you have on when you're shooting the breeze with people and showing them stuff. And then, you know, fluorescent lights, etc., when you actually want to do some work.

I want pools of light in a shed. I want mellowness and contrast and I like the colours and the corners of the shed to kind of fall away into darkness. Sheds are largely winter spaces and it's about feeling cosy, warm and safe, somewhere where I can curl up and snooze if I want to.

Lighting is critical to any room or any place, but with a shed you also have to think about external lighting. If you really want to push the boat out, get yourself a Victorian street lamp to illuminate the path to the shed. It might sound mad, but you can get an original Victorian street lamp for about 300 quid that otherwise is just going to be lost forever. It needs to be blasted and painted; or you can just wire brush it and paint it. It gives a lovely Jack the Ripper, penny-for-the-guy vibe I find.

I wouldn't suggest, by the way, candles. They're very much a no-no in the shed for obvious reasons. I mean, if you want to light a snout, I suppose, on a regular basis, you could light a candle in your shed so you can get your Woodbine in there, and also you might need a lighter to spark up your oxyacetylene torch or whatever. But, you know, please beware, user, you never know. Shed dwellers are grown-ups, though, so I reckon as long as you blow your naked flames out before you toddle off to bed, it should all be cushty.

Lighting is actually key to raising your shed experience from storage facility to tranquil ocean of rejuvenating calm. That's why one of my favourite shed jobs is making new lights. Anything will do as a base but my preferred material is an old petrol can or a random piece of automotive junk.

You just drill a few holes, solder on a fitting and boom, you got a light. I think they're amazing, my homemade lights. One person who disagrees is my wife, Janie. She won't have them in the house.

One area where wives like to get involved in sheds, in my experience, is curtains. I'm a bit worried about curtains in a shed because I immediately see that kind of Cath Kidston look, light blue backing with red roses. I think it's a bit dodgy if your partner makes you some curtains as a present for your new shed. Because then you're verging on it being an extension, aren't you? And that's why curtains make me nervous: the minute curtains go in, you might be sleeping in it, mate. It might be the wife thinking: 'I'm doing curtains, I'll put a telly in it, then I'll put a composting bog in it and then he can clear off and he can live in the shed.' So, beware the woman who brings curtains I say.

6:
Furnishing Your Shed

So you've got your shed up, lit it, painted it and you've hopefully installed two separate circuits for the plugs. Now you need somewhere to rest your arse.

Well, I say, push the boat out and get something mad as your showcase seating. Like, a vintage barber's chair's a really nice thing to have in a shed. It's masculine, it's fun, you're never going to be allowed one in the house and the Sweeney Todd vibe goes a long way to incubating honesty.

A vintage barber's chair is also a good choice because leather is critical as regards shed furnishing. In my new shed I've got a sofa and two chairs, leather covered, that have been made out of old Riley seats, literally car seats that have been made into chairs and a sofa. Now, that's critical levels of shed enjoyment, because making them was a laugh and sitting in them is an actual treat. Leather is critical. It's the smell of it and the feel of it, and the fact that it's the bridge between furnishings and automotive accessories. Funnily enough, leather is seen as de rigueur by the wives now, but I think posh leather misses the point. Its spiritual home really is in a shed, on a Chesterfield button-back sofa with some oil on it. It needs to be split in places and repaired, it needs to have the proper patina of age.

Seating arrangements are a fundamental consideration in

any shed, because as well as having a workspace, your shed needs to have the facility to be a social space. So, you need to make a decision about how hospitable you want your shed to be. A good start is to ask yourself: when someone comes into my shed visiting, will I generally be happy for them to be there for two cups of tea plus, or do I want them to be one cup of tea or under? Your answer to this question will inform your seating, because, just in the same way as McDonald's seem to arrange the seating so that it gets uncomfortable after half an hour so you clear off, you should look at that as regards the seat that you offer the person coming in the shed if, like most of us, you're a one cup socializer.

One trick that I can recommend is always to have a couple of stools in the shed, which I do, and I also have a Ural motorbike seat turned into a stool, which is not uncomfortable if you get it right, but you need to know what you're doing. You can't just sit on it and hope for the best; you'll fall off. You need to hold onto the grab rail at the front and balance yourself nicely. It's a ten to fifteen minute seat.

Padded stools are handy for work as well. You're up against your workbench, yeah, and instead of standing up, you can perch. So, for instance, soldering is always done better sitting on the stool. Don't try and solder loads of things standing up when there's the alternative to have a stool.

Sofas and armchairs in a shed are obviously in no way relevant to the work operations; they're to sit, ponder, look at what's in your shed and reflect. Giving it, as they say, two coats of looking at. I do think a two-seater sofa in your shed is almost pointless. If you're on your own, an armchair is better and if you are going to sit and have a cup of tea with your mate, you're a bit too close on a two-seater, so you're not going to relax. A three-seater sofa is a little less invasive, but two armchairs are the best option really, for blokes who like their personal space.

I really love modifying automotive stuff, so I've got a Jaguar 3.8 rear bench seat and passenger and driver seat converted into a three-piece suite which is pretty incredible. It's even got the central armrest that you pull down still in situ, which does help to define the seats a bit. They smell of old leather, they're beautifully made, they've got this lovely frame around them now, they look vintage, they feel vintage, they smell vintage. That's probably the ultimate shed seating, converted classic car seats.

Leather is obviously the top choice for furnishing finishes in a shed, because you can get the oil off with a rag and some solvent. If you go on Pinterest, the quintessential shed always has a Chesterfield in it and I think that's right. You never see the quintessential shed with a little bit of velour. You never see that. Leather is kind of synonymous with shed-dwelling restoration retro and all that, button backed, ideally, so it's got that old club feel to it and that kind of caper.

Now, truth be told, I actually find them quite uncomfortable. They look amazing but one downside is that they're quite hard and you do slide off, especially in a boiler suit. But a shed sofa isn't built purely for comfort. I mean, you're not going to be lying there for ten hours watching Netflix. The seating in sheds is absolutely different to the seating in the house. In the house, it's like: 'Get the dog off the sofa, darling. What are you doing? Don't put your feet on the sofa.' Well, it all happens in the shed, man. You can put your boots on the sofa, because the wife ain't going to come in and say, 'Clean it.'

Also, if you've got leather, a little bit of Pledge works wonders. Give it a little rub down, and you're done. So the actual outer materials of your seating arrangements in the shed need to be fully washable and hard-wearing. The seats should also not absorb any damp, because the worst thing possible, man, is that you sit on a sofa in another man's shed that the roof has dripped on, and you get a wet arse. You don't want to be in that shed.

So, seating is a fundamental thing when it comes to creating that womb-like atmosphere in a shed. Your chairs have got to be cosy and they've got to reflect a bit of you, which in my case means old motorbike seats turned into stools.

It's actually a very good example of how, creatively, you can have a free rein in the shed, whereas in the house, if the wife wants a Parker Knoll recliner, she's got one. But a Parker Knoll recliner does not sit well in the shed. Why would you have a Parker Knoll in a shed? You recline it, and as you recline, you knock your bike off the workbench. You don't want anything that reclines automatically like that in a shed.

One thing I would strongly endorse in sheds, which I've got into recently, is period deckchairs. Now, when you get yourself a period deckchair, try and make sure that it hasn't been in a wet shed for the past fifty years, cos you don't want it to rot through and get mould cos you'll fall through it, but, if you can eliminate that risk, they're ultimately comfy, and they're aesthetically pleasing if you get the stripy ones. And, check this out: you can sleep in them. The other great thing, obviously, is that they are foldable so they aren't cluttering up the shed when your pal has cleared off. That's the same reason I like old director's chairs; they are eminently foldable. So, you can tuck them away behind your tool chest, but when your mates come by you can bring them out and they're wonderfully comfy.

Now, another amazing thing about them being foldable and tucked behind the tool chest is that you've got plausible deniability when it comes to the seating of the occasional twat who may show up. So, when someone comes into the shed visiting who you don't want to be there, they've got nothing to sit on, which means you can be time sensitive on them. If they come in and go, 'All right, Henry, how are you?' and your first thought is, 'Oh, Christ, it's Malcolm from down the road, all he's got is a bloody C50 Cub moped, and he's got no decent chat,' then just don't get the deckchair out and he'll be gone in ten minutes. But then, you know, when my best mates come round, I can lay out the red carpet. I can get the deckchair out, get the tea out for them, the biscuits.

That's proper nice, isn't it? That's what it's about; your world, your domain and a seating system that gets rid of twats fast. The worst thing possible is to have seating that actually encourages all visitors to perch on it when they come in the shed. The only thing you can do in that case is bolt the shed from the inside. But bolting sheds from the inside is really questionable. The minute you bolt the shed, you are restricting your wife/partner coming in, and then, you know, what are you doing? All these questions start to arise. And then, suddenly, your sacred haven could be taken away from you because your partner believes that you're up to something rude in there. All because you didn't think through your seating.

 ⌐I mean, people should respect the sanctity of the shed, but you have to play your part in that. The respect goes both ways. 'I'm in the shed, but I'm just tinkering and I'm escaping this crazy modern life. Please feel free to come in, partner, because I'm not doing anything naughty.' I mean, I think it's okay to Chubb lock the door if you're sandblasting or something, but generally, you don't want to start locking yourself in the shed.

Do not waste your time putting any flat-pack domestic furniture in a shed. One, it will fall apart; two, that stuff only looks good in houses; and three; in a shed your stuff has got to be sturdy.

So, yes, the shed is an escape, a refuge, a womb and a huge part of it properly being all of those things is that it it's completely yours, and you can design and decorate it however you like. You want carpet on the ceiling? Egg boxes on the walls? A water chair? A slide on the roof? A La-Z-Boy with built-in massage function? Do it, man.

Your wife/partner doesn't get a say on what comes into

your shed or goes on the wall, and wouldn't want one, because what goes on in my shed is not subject to the same laws as what goes on in the house. That's her domain; this is mine. Back in the house, I take orders. Janie runs the house. I put my cup in the dishwasher, take my shoes off and do not drop biscuit crumbs on the sofa. Also, I can't wheel a motorbike into the kitchen, but I most definitely can wheel one into my shed. And Janie would never want stuff that I restore in the house. Those lovely lamps I've been working on? They're for sheds as far as she's concerned.

I can keep a cow in it. I can try and grow bananas in it. I can watch silent movies, and maybe play along on the piano. I can do whatever I want in my shed (except view pornography, as per Commandment Three, because it's bad for the soul).

Shed world and house world are mutually exclusive. Anything which could cause a rift between you and your partner – just do it in the shed, son. The house is Janie's. But my shed is mine. There's very few times in life where you and only you can decide the environment that you're going to stand and sit in. This is one of them, don't waste it.

Anthropologically what is interesting is that when you have your own environment of a shed, you then often find a lot of blokes can't stop once they've started and, having created one world, they create another world within that in the form of a model railway or a Scalextric or something like that, so, that's the double whammy of shed joy.

One thing that upsets me in a shed is a freebie calendar

on the wall from a parts or metalwork supplier that isn't up to date. If it's April and the calendar is still on March, that really annoys me. It speaks of an unseriousness of purpose, because in any restoration, or indeed any wider iteration of shed dwelling, the attention is in the detail.

Calendars I don't actually find too useful, but what I do like is a whiteboard gridded up into a year-planner, month-by-month wallchart that you can use to map out a build programme. It's useful if you can have your white-board big enough that there is space for scribbling down stuff that's missing that you need to get, or just general notes along the lines of 'Must pick the kids up from school at three'.

But the annual wallchart is a vital tool. I actually can't think straight if I don't have a wallchart. I can't make any plans. It's commensurate with age; the older you get, the more you need a wallchart. I've got the memory span of a gnat these days, so I almost need to have 'Eat lunch at one' on my wallchart. Without a wallchart one forgets one's life. The wallchart is cool as well because it is a bit of a fantasy life. It's you if you were perfect and everything happened on time and you never forgot your anniversary.

But fundamentally the wallchart and the wall list are really valuable tools when you're doing a build. Like, I'm doing a build at the moment, so up on the chart for next week I've got 'Re-align brakes, get front-end nickel-plated, need sparkplugs'. Now, that's pretty basic info but unless I get that stuff done next week I can't go onto the next stage and I'm just not going to remember the minute details about needing the rear hub getting laced unless I catalogue it on a wall list.

When I have done something on the list, I don't rub it off, I just tick it. Now, obviously, there comes a point when you need to rub it all off and make a clean sweep but in the meantime it's nice to reflect on what you have managed to get done and understand that you're getting somewhere. There's a sense of achievement if you go, 'Oh yeah, I cleaned the carbs, I reset the timing belt.' Then you can tick it off and it looks as though you're really going for it, firing ahead. It's good for morale and morale is vital in a shed.

The wallchart, I feel, is all about keeping some sense of control of your environment. Now, I know that we are all meant to chill out and not be so controlling, etc., but that doesn't really apply in a shed setting. You need to be on top of your brief, and that means knowing where everything is, and knowing how far along in a project you are.

One part of furnishing your shed I haven't touched on yet is carpet. My mate Tom has a shed with carpet on the walls, which I have to say I find a bit alarming.

Before they invented digital, I used to spend a fair bit of my time in recording studios or film-to-video transfer places, and one of them had red shag pile carpet all over the floors, walls and ceilings, including in the lavatory, and I think going into a 360-degree carpeted shed gives me flashbacks.

Now, obviously, if you're doing music or something in your shed, you're gonna need all that caper but I don't necessarily think it's a great way to go about making your shed womb-like for the rest of us. The womb-like thing is emotional, rather than physical, that's the point.

Now, just to contradict myself, I have sometimes wondered about putting carpet on the ceiling when I had a shed with a tin roof, because when it rained in that shed it felt as if the world was going to cave in. Even the slightest shower, the noise was like a load of military marching down the road and it was genuinely quite terrifying.

The main reason, however, that I would demur from the tendency to put carpet on the walls and ceilings goes back to my abiding feeling that you want your shed to be above suspicion. Because the thing is, one needs to make sure that your shed, both outwardly and inwardly, doesn't appear to be being used for anything untoward. The moment you go round putting a bolt on the inside of the door and carpeting the walls, anyone who comes in thinks, 'What's he going to get up to in here?'

Yet another reason I wouldn't want to carpet the inside of my shed is because the whole beauty of a shed is the wooden walls.

And also you need to think about how carpet might impact shelving; you need a lot of shelving in a shed. But if you're going to carpet it, that's going to create complications when it comes to putting up shelves because they aren't going to be flush up against the wood, are they? They are going to have half a centimetre of carpet weakening them. So you're either going to have to do the carpet in strips, or you are not going to have anything on the walls, because if you're not going to have anything on the walls then, well, you shouldn't really be in a shed, should you? You might as well be outside or in a tent or something.

I don't really go for that student, opium den vibe in my sheds, with tie-dyed drapes and all that kind of stuff. I mean, for me a shed is fundamentally a place to be getting on with your endeavour first; while sitting around smoking opium (or more likely drinking tea these days) may be important, chilling should be the secondary function of the shed, not its primary purpose, or it loses its integrity.

One of the things I love about my sheds is that they are full of stuff that often has no value for anyone else but are among my most treasured possessions in the world. For instance, my mate John made me a little framed board with nine different Royal Enfield Redditch spanners pinned to it. I mean, who would have thought of that? That is something that I truly cherish. What's it worth? Nothing. Absolutely nothing. Okay – maybe eight quid on a good day if you got lucky at the auto jumble. But it's one of the most valuable things I own. And that is what shed dwelling is all about. It's about making this little world that is your own utopia, and if other people can't understand that, then stuff them.

I'm a big proponent of recycling and reusing stuff, and that includes brown furniture. Since about the mid-1980s, when people suddenly realized they could go to Ikea, which was just starting out, and get perfectly decent stuff for nothing, the price of brown furniture, as the experts call that heavy, antique furniture, fell off a cliff.

I go, on a regular basis, to massive big sheds full of

brown furniture, all of which is now essentially worthless because no one wants it. My father, being an antique dealer, bequeathed me a load of that stuff when he died, all of which is basically very desirable woodworm accommodation now.

But there is a movement now, of which I'm one of the protagonists, which is about taking all that proper but worthless stuff, like Victorian sideboards, chests of drawers, dining room tables, and repurposing them. I bolt pillar drills to them and turn them into workbenches, or paint and distress them to create shed storage which has a retro feel. That's very much a movement right now; what we're doing is, we're sanding back the drawers or even taking the veneers and the marquetry off and rattle-canning them matt black and putting industrial handles on them.

On the one hand it's sacrilege, but on the other, we're actually creating workbenches and storage facilities from these worthless bits of Victorian brown wood that are cheap, accessible and also look sort of retro and cool. Once you get over the fact that these beautiful old things are going to actually be worth more even if you had them as workbenches rather than side tables – that perhaps, you know, it's the price of progress – then you can really have some fun with it. I mean, there's nothing sadder than those things sitting in a damp shed decaying.

I go into thousands of sheds with all this stuff piled high when actually, with a little bit of creativity and a little bit of ingenuity, you can create something *in* the shed *for* the shed with it. An awful lot of people are making it worth something again. That brown furniture lends itself beautifully to a custom chop shop or a bike restoration company because it makes the workshop look so cool and established. I'd really recommend it as a beginner's shed project; strip off the marquetry and the carvings and get a rattle can out. If it doesn't work out, burn it; it's only the same price as firewood anyway.

7:
Shelving and
Mental Health

Every time I buy a new bike, I recall the old adage, 'Know thy beast', which basically means, 'Go and ride that bike for a hundred miles, and work out what goes wrong.' Find out if she'll start only when she's hot, or if you need to leave her to cool down for a sec, rather than kicking away like crazy for hours.

It's just the same with a shed. You need to know thy shed. Which basically means you need to know where everything is. So, at the end of every day, however much you can't be arsed, however late it is, try and clear up and put everything back in its place because you'll reap the benefits the next day. Tidiness and order are absolutely vital, and to be honest it makes a nice contrast to all that crazy chaos that surrounds us in the everyday world.

It's nice to come into the shed, take a deep breath and just know how it's going to be. Because the frustration that you will feel when you've got a brake hub that won't come apart, and you're looking for your hub puller, and you can't find it just because you didn't put it back in its home is unimaginable.

Then, go one step further where are you going to vent

that frustration? On that brake hub with a hammer and a screwdriver. The frustration, the mental and spiritual cataclysmic depression that takes over when you can't do something because you couldn't be bothered yesterday to put something back in its place is, I think, so incredibly frustrating precisely because it's all your fault.

There is no satisfaction in that kind of shed life whatsoever, and if you have a can't-be-bothered attitude you will ruin your own environment, which is a long way of saying you've got to clear up and you've got to put the tools back. It does require you to be controlling and pernickety and that's okay if you can remember to leave that attitude in the shed and go back to the house and not yell at the kids because they have left their iPads down the back of the sofa again.

But, honestly, the state of your toolbox is a pretty accurate gauge for your state of mind. Is everything where it should be? No? Then get into a shed with a mate and figure out what's wrong, man, because if you don't do that, you are actually going to have a miserable time in the shed. Proper miserable. Because there'll be no satisfaction and contentment, you know? None.

Now, the first question any shed man has to think about is whether he should draw an outline of each tool on the wall around the nail on which it hangs. Now, originally, those tool outlines on a wall were relevant to workshops which loads of people used, because, you know, if you had Louie and Pip with you working in the shed, then they would know at the end of the day to put your adjustable spanner in the right outline. But to have it in a shed that only one man uses suggests that he is chronically untidy, and unfortunately chronic untidiness has no place in a shed.

The world is so chaotic, that most shed dwellers like their sheds to be temples of order, almost to the extent that they've got a bit of OCD going on. That's certainly the case for me. My tools are kept in drawers, and they are properly sorted.

Drawer one: left of the tool cabinet, I have the socket sets. Drawer two: metric spanners. Drawer three: UNF imperial spanners. Top drawer right: screwdrivers. Underneath that: pliers, side cutters, verniers, all that kind of caper. Underneath that a selection of hammers and then underneath that you've got pulling tools, then you're into your saws, you know, your hacksaws, and all that.

So, what I'm saying to you is that instead of cut-outs (that, I have to admit, do look cool), actually, if you're in touch with your OCD in a good way and you're the only person in the shed, then a tool chest is the way forward.

Double stacking tools is not cool because to absolutely know where everything is, you have to be able to see it too. And double stacking leads inevitably to triple stacking. And the worst thing in a shed, right, the thing that will put people off restoring stuff, is knowing you have the right tool but not being able to find it.

If someone lets you use their shed or their toolbox, therefore, put things back. Shed law allows for a death sentence on people who leave tools in different places in someone else's shed. You don't put tools back, you're a dead man. It's so annoying when you just can't find the tool and it's always the one you need to finish the job. That's why you need to be aware that when you give someone the keys to your shed, that is basically like giving him keys to a chastity belt. So when the question is asked: 'Can I borrow your shed, mate? I know you're going out tonight.' The answer is, 'No. You can't. Because you are going to take all my tools out and put them back in the wrong place.'

If you're not a tidy person naturally, you can still become a more disciplined person within the shed, and this is what's so fantastic about the possibility for very measurable spiritual growth in a shed. Because you may be totally laissez-faire in the kitchen, you may leave your side plate that had your Marmite on toast on and your cup with Ovaltine dregs in on the side of the sink and think, 'I'll get it later', but in a shed you're paring it all down to the absolute minimum and you're just thinking, 'When I finish with this screwdriver, I'm going to put it back in the screwdriver drawer.' And you do it once, and you're away, you're on the road and before you know it the shed has become a clean place, a place that's cleaner than your kitchen, because it's your shed, not the family's. It's your environment and in your environment best practice becomes adhered to.

If a shed is filthy and disorganised and unloved, you are just bankrupt, spiritually. But if you go the other way, part of that is taking care of your tools. The satisfaction you get from knowing you have every single tool that you're going to need to switch out a transfer box in a mellow and understanding way is blissful. But if you are trying to free up a bolt, but desperately looking for WD-40 and you can't find it and then you attack it, you will muller it because you're totally frustrated before you start. And you'll end up burring the bolt and then having to angle-grind it off, because you're just ranting angrily at the world.

The order of a shed is the total juxtaposition to the chaos that you face in everyday life. And it's about all the good parts of a life without children. Just in the sense that for a lot of us who have kids, our only place of peace is the shed. You love them to bits, of course, but they are not allowed in the shed, and although we pretend it's because they are going to hurt themselves, it's really because they are going to pick stuff up from one place and put it down in another place and then you won't be able to find it. There's nothing helpful about having a child in a shed. There's nothing good. And also you can recharge your batteries in the child-free environs of the shed to be a better father.

A key element of any shed is the shelving. You want your shelving to be sturdy, which is another reason I recommend no less than 45mm thick walls, because otherwise they can't take any halfway heavy shelving. There's nothing worse than a shelf falling off a wall in a shed. It's got to be strong. You don't want to be thinking, 'Oh, I better not drill through this,' or 'I don't know whether this will support that.' Shed stuff is monster heavy, so the shelving needs to be robust and the walls have to be robust too.

The best shelving, I think, is cubbyhole shelving. Let's

discuss it for a moment. I don't really think you can get very far in a shed without cubbyhole shelving. Cubbyhole shelving is like your brain rendered into physical storage. Without cubbyhole shelving, you will go and buy new parts for a motorbike and then you realize, six months later, that you had them all along. But if all your parts are stored in properly managed cubbyhole shelving, that is not a mistake you are going to make.

Yes, it saves you wasting money but more importantly it also makes you feel like a man in control of his own life when you can go, 'Hmm, spokes, I am sure I have some of them round here, somewhere – ah yes, here they are,' rather than going, 'I know I've got some spokes in the shed somewhere but I haven't a clue where. I'll order some new ones online.'

Knowing where things are is part of the mental discipline of the shed. And to me, aesthetically, cubbyhole shelves are just the most beautiful things, right? Because they give a sense of excitement to the most boring of all known tasks: filing. Cubbyhole shelving is a nice thing to see when you walk into another man's shed too. Visually you're looking at cubbyhole shelving on a wall thinking, 'I wonder what's in there? Well, I can just have a look. God, he's got some incredible vintage bulbs here, I didn't know he was into those,' or, 'Wow! I'd love a whole load of wire brushes like that.' Life, as you get older, is all about the simple things. It's like, 'Oh, man, I'm going to sit in bed tonight and plan where my wire brushes are going to go in my new cubby-hole shelving.'

You discover, via cubbyhole shelving, an interest in things that you would never believe that you could be interested in. Brass knobs. Brake levers. Seat springs. I've got millions of seat springs but I wanted ones a little bit longer than usual yesterday, for my Harley. And suddenly, thanks to cubbyhole shelving, I've got some springs. I try not to hoard junk but I do have one special cubbyhole for unidentified objects that will one day be identified. It's an open filing system for objects, and filing for your brain as well.

I really like the former army cubbyhole shelving units, not least because they are insanely durable and they usually cost about thirty quid because idiotic people who do not value the heritage of this country are literally throwing away stuff like this. They're proper bellends, those people. They have no idea of what actually is lovely in this world and they are what's wrong with society. To think that cubbyhole shelving, what it's seen, what it's been through, what heritage it has, means nothing to them. They are part of the throwaway society, and us old geezers, well, actually we're in our sheds and no, we're not throwing stuff away, we're keeping stuff because we think we may well need it to reinvigorate our national heritage at some stage down the line.

Cubbyhole shelving is all about looking after your needs, not your wants. It's about something really simple: having all your tools, all your chargers or your spirit levels to hand, in order and off the workbench. It's about having everything you actually need, and the reason why this world's so messed up is that people aren't content to be just looking after their needs, because their needs are catered for, and so they are moving on to wants. So, they want their wants and when they want their wants, right, well, they are never going to be satisfied.

Like, I've got an old battery charger, which normally some goon would just throw away despite the fact that it works absolutely fine, just because he cannot be bothered to clean the contact points. Well, I'll use that rather than buying a new one, any day of the week, and it'll work great and it will put the electricity into the battery.

I think it's a mini tragedy every time something that is or was once useful is chucked out, whether it's a grease gun with a patent number on it or an old lantern, but the problem is we have lost touch not just with fixing stuff but with keeping stuff going. This is a part of shed dwelling, getting stuff like this, having a look at it and thinking about it and ideally, one day, using it. Getting it going. Working out how it works, what it was used for. That's shed dwelling and shed chat. Like, I have an old jump seat from a Second World War II transport plane. I like to imagine Smithers bolting it to the floor and off we'd go for a sortie over Dresden.

The laziness and stupidity of non-shed dwellers gives us the opportunity to clean up, of course. I bought an Aston Martin liveried petrol pump for four grand the other day. Four grand! For a pivotal piece of British automotive history?! It's insane.

People just can't be arsed to do anything any more. And that's why us lot are different. Sheds are about endeavour. They're about restoration: spiritually, mentally and physically. And it doesn't matter what you restore as long as you are passionate about it. One guy I know has a shed full of old vintage railway signalling equipment and he is one of the most contented people on the planet.

8:
Attaining Tool Nirvana

So, what about your kit? A few essential tools I would suggest kitting your shed out with from day one include a vice, which is just a brilliant thing to have, and hard to do much without. I would suggest going for a soft jaws vice, so basically when you're clamping something, you don't make lines on it. So, a vice is critical. A socket set is also critical. And a selection of spanners and screwdrivers and a hammer. It's amazing really how few tools you actually need.

I mean, two of the greatest mechanics I think in the world are Allen Millyard and Sam Lovegrove (my respective partners-in-crime on the TV shows *Find It, Fix It, Flog It* and *Shed and Buried*) and they both turn up with minuscule toolboxes. Your tools reduce in direct proportion to your experience and skill. The more experienced you are, the less tools you require. So, someone like me, who is an amateur mechanic, I'm just going crazy online, just buying everything. I can't help myself. Add to basket, add to basket, make an offer, add to basket, thanks very much, I'm having it. Right? So, consequently, I've got sheds filled with mirrors on sticks that you can look behind crevices with, I've got magnetic extendable things, I've got offset screwdrivers, I've got kinked screwdrivers. I've got clutch pullers, I've got hub pullers, I've got some of those suction cups for lifting up glass that I never need to pick up. I've got every single size spanner ever made; I've got imperial, I've got Whitworth, I've got everything. And then when Sammy turns up, he's got about four spanners.

You mustn't confuse experience, with owning more and more tools, because my experience is you can have all the gear and no idea. It's like the kid who turns up at the skatepark with a smashed up skateboard and one pair of Billabong pants is always the best. I mean, it's properly amazing what Sam can do with a chisel. The big tool is the one up in your head, and until you've figured out how to use that one, the others ain't no use to you.

There is a lot of truth in the old saying that a bad workman blames his tools, but the real truth is that a brilliant craftsman has the right tools (because if you have the wrong tool for the job, and you're going to try and change a tyre with two screwdrivers, then you're an idiot and you're going to scratch the rim and puncture the inner tube) but the genius workman doesn't need very many of them.

You do need a few power tools and if you've got an angle grinder or something like that, make it battery powered. A flex gets caught up, and if your motorbike's sitting outside or something, you can just pick up the whizzy wheel and out you go and it's on battery.

But when it comes to hand tools, less is more. Buy two screwdrivers of the best quality rather than twenty of poor quality. You don't realize until you get going in a shed, how critical good quality hand tools are.

If you buy a socket set for thirty quid, all they're going to do is drive you mad. They're not going to fit the bolts properly, they're going to chafe and wear away the corners and the damage that you can wreak with bad tools is just insane. Let's say you've got a prized Royal Enfield and then you go and set about it with your crappy socket set and burr off the nuts. Well, you're just going to hate yourself. Treat your bike to decent tools, because it is the love of your life, and just like your wife, it could kill you at any moment if you don't ride it properly.

You need to make sure that whatever tools you have are either within, or will soon be within, your talent zone. There's no point in using a vernier, which is used for measuring the inside dimensions of holes, down to microns, unless you know how to use it and what to do with the information once you've acquired it.

So pick your tools carefully, read up on them and enjoy that experience of breaking new ground. Honestly, if you're not learning, you shouldn't be in a shed. Go down the pub for recreation.

One thing I love is when I go into another man's shed and they've got a tool that I've never seen before. What a lovely conversation point that is: 'What do you use that for?' There's a bit of vulnerability required in asking that, but risk a little emotionally and ask anyway, and you're going to get such good advice.

So when it comes to tools, you do need the right tools,

you need the best quality tools, but you don't need millions of them. Tools are one of the defining features of humanity, according to anthropologists. There's something just amazing about tools, about the fact that somebody's sat down with this problem and created something to solve it.

Sometimes, I see Sam or Allen working on something and I go, 'What are you doing? Welding that? I thought you were just going to take the head off, you don't need to weld it.' 'No, no, Henry, I'm making a tool.' 'What?' I say. 'I'm making a tool to use to get the head off without cracking it.' 'Oh, are you? Okay.'

You see, I'd have just got a screwdriver, stuck it in the gasket, twisted it, wrecked the lip on the seal and broken everything when actually they are making a tool to get the brake hubs off. Just welding up a tool. That to me is just the expression of the greatest part of mankind, each man doing his job and doing it right. Just getting stuff right.

So, that's tools dealt with. But what else? One key thing that is often overlooked when stocking a shed, and which can make your life glorious, is getting the right solvents. Everyone always goes, 'I need the right tools,' but trust me, if you haven't got a can of brake cleaner and you haven't got a can of WD-40, and you haven't got a can of penetrating oil and you haven't got methylated spirits and white spirit in the shed, well, there's no point in going. Forget it. Don't even get out of bed, mate.

What you need to do is, you need to be in control of your solvents. Let's say, for instance, you've got oil on an enamel sign and loads of grime and detritus. What are you going to get it off with? Well, the worst thing possible is to use something that will actually mess the paint up or the enamel. So, you need to get progressively more aggressive with your cleaning options. So initially I always use furniture polish spray like Pledge or Mr Sheen. It blows my mind how effectively Pledge gets rid of oil and dirt. It's amazing, and also it's guaranteed not to hurt the paint underneath, whether it's a petrol can or a tin sign.

Autosol is great for polishing stuff. It's slightly abrasive, and it's a cream that comes out of a tube like a toothpaste. That is the best polishing medium. Then, next up, make sure you get yourself a can of brake cleaner. It is amazing to clean metal up, just unbelievably brilliant. I don't know why it's called brake cleaner, it should be called 'everything cleaner' because it really does clean everything.

Also another trick, if the oil and grime is really impregnable, use Cif. The stuff that they clean baths with, formerly known as Jif. It'll take it off, guaranteed.

If you peel a sticker off a window and it leaves a residue, the solvent you are after is methylated spirits or white spirit. Let's have it, son. It'll come off.

Also there are two other requisites that you need in a shed in connection with solvents. The first thing is blue roll, it's like industrial strength bog paper and it's blue-coloured. I use tons of it. And the other thing is muslin rag. Yeah? You get rolls of muslin. Don't even go in your shed if you haven't got any muslin. You get it on the Internet or at any motor factors. I use yards of it on a daily basis in my shed. Those are the two rags you need.

Now, with all this wrangling and solvent use and spanners and tools, get yourself a comfy chair. Honestly. If you're polishing something, and you're not in a comfy chair polishing it, it's not going to be a pleasant experience because you'll just want to finish as quickly as possible. If you're in a comfy chair and you're warm, you're going to do a better job of cleaning the sprogget washer, you know? If you're freezing cold, you don't want to be there, so you're going to go, 'Oh, that'll do,' and leave the job half-finished. During a restoration in a shed the phrase not to use is 'That'll do'. That's the ultimate sin. Because the minute you say that once on a restoration – 'Oh that'll do' – you'll say it a thousand times after it and the resto will look like garbage. The devil is in the detail in everything that you do in a shed, and the moment you start cutting a corner, you're finished, because you're just going to do it again.

When you're talking about serious tools for serious restoration jobs, then pulleys are a great thing to have in a shed. I love the ingenuity of them – they are a great way to use height, if you have it. Serious enthusiasts will often have a great big pulley for getting an engine out of a car but a set of smaller pulleys comes in very handy if you want a model railway; you can lower it down from the ceiling, do a bit of work on it or play with it, or whatever, and then wind it back up again to get your bike on the stand.

When I lived in London, I had a pulley system in the garage for Scalextric and model railways and there's something very satisfying about the way a pulley allows you to have multiple hobbies in a shed. Some model railway enthusiasts even have it arranged so they can sit there in the middle of their garage and use the pulley system to drop the diorama around them, because there's a hole cut in the big bit of hardwood for them to sit in. So, you kind of encase yourself in your hobby, but when you go to the auction and you buy a Velocette 350 and you want to restore it, then you can hoist everything up.

The opposite to a pulley, in some respects, is an inspection pit. I have to say that to have an inspection pit, ideally one that's covered over with wooden flooring, is the *sine qua non* of shed excellence – and really not at all expensive to build if you plan it that way first. It really is incredible how much you can learn when you get under your old 2CV with a hand-held lamp in an inspection pit in your own shed, and it's actually way cheaper and more manageable than a car lift. Obviously, if you're going to have a car lift, however cool they are, your shed's got to be absolutely massive and really high, and very few people have a tall shed. So dig down, man. Make like a mole. An inspection pit concealed within your shed? That's living the dream!

When you get into an inspection pit, just with five minutes of someone telling you what's what, you can quickly understand a basic car. It definitely beats lying on the road looking under your vehicle, and it also means that you don't need loads of space around the car; with a pit, it doesn't matter if the car's right in against the walls. Get in your inspection pit, son, and you are away.

And also it's quite a nice cosy place to be actually. You're hidden away from the world. The wife ain't gonna be able to find you. I mean, I don't know if you want to get into sitting down there with a cup of tea on a regular basis, but it is actually a surprisingly easy and cheap way to bring a whole other dimension to your shed, that just requires a little planning.

The other nice thing about inspection pits is that they are totally safe. You can put as much pressure as you want on that prop shaft and the car ain't gonna fall on you. Speaking of that, one bit of advice: if it's too late to go down the inspection pit road, don't skimp on your jack. Buy the biggest jack you can afford. I'll tell you what, man, when you're underneath the car and a gust of wind catches it, you'll think, 'I'm really pleased I bought that big jack.' And I do not recommend bottle jacks. I'm always a bit scared of them. They could go at any moment. But in an inspection pit, you know that the car's not going to fall on you and kill you and that's very reassuring. It's just such a nice feeling.

Having an inspection pit is a good way to do what you need to do when you're doing a restoration, which is to take out the variables. And so, if you take out the variables along the way like not being worried about the jack because you've got your inspection pit, you can then concentrate on the job in hand. Because there is always that moment when you're under a car that is on a jack, and you're wrenching a nut that won't come off, and you think, 'Might this thing fall on me?' If you're in your inspection pit, your mind is 100 per cent on getting that nut off, with as much force as you can. You can use as many crowbars as you want, you know? It doesn't matter how hard you pull it. You're not going to die.

9:
Mental Rehab

The shed is the place to regenerate the soul. It's the place to take a risk. It's the place to make mistakes because no one's there. It's like, you know, how they say if a tree falls in the forest did it actually make a noise if no one was there to hear it? Well, if you mess up a carburettor and no one's there, and then you fix it the next day, did you mess it up? I really don't think so. A shed is a good, safe place to take a risk, to test your abilities and in my opinion that is the only way you grow as a human being.

The really important thing about a shed being your own private empire where you run rigorous border control is that it means it's a safe place to make mistakes. I often break things in the shed when I'm trying to fix them. Last Boxing Day, just to get out of the house, I stripped the carburettor out of a working bike, cleaned it, put it back together and the thing wouldn't start. Didn't matter. Happened in the shed.

The allowance of mistakes is, I think, the reason why almost anything that's any good, mechanically speaking, has been invented in a shed. Sheds do genuinely foster a very literal and practical kind of creativity and that's why everything in this world that is worth anything, mechanically-wise, has been invented in a shed. I mean, think about it. The motor, the electric light bulb, the telephone. Sheds, sheds, sheds.

Er, probably. Who needs a great big working environment and a factory and all that kind of stuff? A factory is for mass-production. A shed is for one-offs.

Ironically, for such a confined space, a shed is very conducive to intellectual and emotional freedom and that includes the freedom to get it wrong. Look at Burt Munro, the New Zealander motorcycle racer who set the under-1,000cc world record, at Bonneville, on 26 August 1967, which still stands. He worked in a shed. Did it all in a shed. Munro was sixty-eight and was riding a forty-seven-year-old machine when he set his last record. How many mistakes did he make in his shed on that path? Hundreds.

You see, if you're going to break the world land speed record, or if you are going to design the best cabinet, or you're going to come up with the ultimate model train layout, you actually need mistakes. Mistakes are the most amazing things, and I keep telling my kids this. If you make the same mistake, you're not learning. But if you make different mistakes, it's called education, it's called lessons in life. You can make mistakes in sheds and the ramifications of those mistakes aren't as bad as having a mega overhead and running before you can walk.

The other thing you need is time, and to have time you need low overheads. And to have low overheads, you need to be in a shed. You need peace, tranquillity and emotional stability, but most of all you need time, and if you are doing whatever you are doing with a team of thirty in a horrible brand-new warehouse, that's costing you three grand a week, you are under pressure, and you're also under pressure to get it right straight away. For creativity to burgeon, to make things, you need to make mistakes without them derailing the whole project and blowing the budget, and that is why sheds are such unbelievably creative places.

I think a shed is a great environment to run a business in. If you're immediately governed by your massive overhead of your office block in Soho or something like that – and I've been there, I know – every corporate decision that you're going to make is relevant to sustaining that overhead. If you're operating from a shed, it's like operating a carefree corporate existence. So, consequently you can create in a shed. You can sit in your little shed and you can spend an extra two weeks developing your creative idea because you've got no massive overhead to pay for.

And also, I find that people that work with me and have done, a lot of them, for many years, enjoy the shed dwelling experience because it's alternative. I think a lot of my staff would not like to work in an open-plan office with touchy people who are preparing to backstab them at any opportunity.

A shed is a safe place for you to be creative or for you to aspire to create a small business empire. That's what a shed is all about. It's a place where you can expand your creativity. It's a place where there's no panic to pay the man. What do you need in the shed to be creative? A packet of Ginger Nuts and a cup of tea. You're sorted, man. You're living the dream.

I bet you Warren Buffett operated from a shed at some point, do you know what I mean? If you're a massive economist, wheeler-dealer, market trader, you just need a computer and a shed and a bit of peace and quiet. That's why you've got to run a business at home from a shed, not from an extension. If you have it in an extension, with a door to the house, your kids are going to come in and disturb you. Your wife's going to pop in and suddenly say, 'Do you want to go out for dinner tonight with all these friends?' Now, if the kids had to walk through the garden in the pissing rain to come and see their father at work, well, that stops my children coming, and then I can do a decent day's work. And that's why a shed, a corporate shed, should be detached. People won't pop in. Especially your family.

To use a motorcycling adage, if you want to get somewhere, and it's a rocky road, you need to be ready for that to take as long as it takes, because if you rush it, you'll come off. So you're going to create the next Fender Stratocaster? Great – do it in a shed, mate, because it's going to take two years, minimum.

These people who go out and get all their investment, I mean, good luck to them, but it's hard to be truly creative under that kind of pressure because you can't take risks. Actually you just need to get a mate, someone who you really get on well with, probably someone who you found in your shed, and get started.

If you want to build a beach buggy or if you want to restore beautiful petrol pumps and convert them to electric charging points (my latest wheeze, as it happens), that is going to happen in a shed. It happens in a shed because there's freedom of expression, there's no overhead, and there's the ability to just take your own sweet time on it, to go to work as normal but come back in the evenings and develop your great idea in private. Sheds are fantastic incubators of inventions.

And because it's not all happening in the house, and you haven't got bits of petrol pump all over the dining room table and the vicar's coming round for tea and the wife's kicking off because she's got a compressor propping up the side table, no one minds or gets pissed off with you.

Go to your shed and you can develop your passion and that is how sheds can also lead to your dream career. So, you can go and do your job during the day, right, as a pest controller or whatever it may be, but let's say you have always dreamt of getting into jewellery-making. Well, you can get in your little shed when you get home, you can make some jewellery, and over time you can get it right, rather than rushing it. Then, once it's right, you go and present it to some buyers and suddenly it might be, if you're passionate enough and clever enough, that you can tell the pest company to stick their job where the sun don't shine.

There's a whole website, Etsy, which I believe is largely flogging the product of sheds. It's unbelievable, Etsy. I sell stuff on it the whole time. It's all people in sheds making the most brilliant stuff. Some guy selling those old granny trays that have a beanbag underneath them, but cool ones, made of leopard print, for your laptop in bed. Girls doing cool jewellery, hand-knitted socks, wooden iPad cases, lamps made by me. It's all going on in sheds. These people, you can tell, a lot of them, that they're on the cusp. They're thinking, 'I can make that, I can do it. I can sell these lamps for twenty-three quid and they only cost me five to make. Maybe I could sack off my job in M&S next year.'

Spending time in a shed is about mental rehabilitation. And that rehabilitation is not complicated, it simply consists of slowly but surely getting in touch with the real me. The shed is just the vehicle which takes me away from the daily worries, and replaces all those problems with much simpler questions like: is today the day that battery is going to turn up? Because if it does, then tonight, after the wife has taken herself up to bed, I can come into the shed with a cup of tea, and it's going to be all nice and warm and I can immerse myself, completely commit myself spiritually, mentally and physically to changing the battery on my Healey.

Now, if you want an hour's worth (well, probably two, knowing me) of contemplation and spiritual contentment, then the satisfaction of fitting a new battery in your Healey, sparking it up and seeing the goddamn thing run is hard to beat.

And it's not even really about the battery. It's about taking yourself to another dimension: utopia, a Holy Grail. Having a shed is deeply symbolic; it's about having a physical and spiritual place to go in life, a place where you are open to learning, to gain more in your chosen hobby or even, potentially, profession. And this is an important point. You can certainly work in a shed – but only if the thing you're doing feels like fun. The shed is a place of serenity and joy, and if you can get a job out of that, nice one mate. In my case, this means restoring old vehicles. The morning I wake up and go, 'Oh no, I have to go to the shed and change the brakes on that Honda,' then that's the moment to sell everything and check into the old folks' home.

And, you know, it's horses for courses. I was in a shed the other day, and, peering out the window, I saw another one. I said: 'What's in that shed?' The geezer went, 'You can't go in there, mate.' 'Oh, right, fair enough,' I said. But then later, I'd sort of won his trust, and he said, 'Okay, you can have a look through the window into the other shed.' So I looked through the window, and saw his collection of Daleks. Right? So don't think that every shed has an old motorbike in it.

It's very important in that kind of situation to compliment the shed as you go in. Even if it's full of Daleks, you know? 'That's a nice Dalek. Wow, really, is that remote control that one? How long did it take you to collect all these? You must have gone all over the world.' Even if it's the biggest pile of horse manure you've ever seen.

I went to another shed recently. Belonged to this bloke, Ken. He went, 'Do you want to come into my big shed?' I went, 'Of course, Ken. Let's have a rummage.' So he threw open the doors, a massive smile on his face, and said, 'What do you reckon? This is what they call breweryana!' And there were rows and rows of free-standing shelves with Johnnie Walker Red Label paraphernalia on them: tumblers, glasses, jugs, ashtrays. Thousands of them. All Johnnie Walker. From old pubs. Totally worthless. Magic.

Not every shed, of course, is worth going into and one solid negative marker is that as you're approaching a shed for the first time, you see white goods in the garden. You see that, I tell you right now, the shed's going to be a terrible scene of woe. There's no point even going in. Make an excuse and turn on your heel at the first sign of a broken fridge because that person has no pride in their accoutrements. Run away, because otherwise you're going to have to issue a fake compliment about his soul-destroying tat.

Another red flag is the mega-shed. Size-wise, a shed shouldn't be able to fit more than one car, or two motorbikes (one on the bench, one on the ground), in it at one time. Building a second, third or fourth shed is usually a much better idea than building a mega-shed. A mega-shed has got no soul. If the shed is too big, it becomes a barn, and in a barn, you're going to feel vulnerable. I have been into sheds where the geezer's got sixty tanks. And that's when things go wrong. People who abuse their sheddery.

I'll never forget one guy who showed us into his smallest shed. There were about eight cars in it, including a Bentley Blower, a Lagonda, a Ferrari and an Austin-Healey. Amazing. Probably four to five million quid's worth of cars in there. So great. That's his shed, where he spends all his time, right.

But then, out the back, I see these . . . warehouses. Great big industrial units. 'What's in there, mate?' I say. 'Oh, nothing I want to sell, boys.' 'Can we take a look anyway?' 'Er, okay.' So off we go. It's maybe 165 feet long, 65 feet wide. And there are, maybe, a hundred Jaguars in there – 3.8s, saloons, lots of other classic cars, Ford Populars. He goes, 'Yeah, I drove all those cars in there and parked them up. I collect them.' Well, he may have driven them in, but the only way they are coming out is with a grab because every single one is rusted through. He has done *nothing* to them. They are done. Every single one of them is *totally done.* It's sacrilege.

But even worse, we go into the next shed which is probably half the size of the first one, and it has got racking and racking and racking filled with NOS – that's 'new old stock' – spare parts from the fifties and sixties for classic cars, exhaust manifolds, headlights, carburettors, everything. There are two huge great holes in the ceiling. Water is pouring in and rusting everything. The floor is covered in beautiful oil cans and old petrol pumps. All lying in the mud. I look at him and I say, 'Mate, what about all these parts?' He goes, 'Oh, I don't want to sell any of that.' 'Well, what are you doing with it?' He goes, 'Oh, I might need them one day.' No, you won't mate, I think. You're eighty. You're not going to need them. All you've done is stopped a whole load of people who were looking for these original parts from being able to buy them. You've just screwed it on a mega scale. For thousands of people. Probably two million quid's worth of parts, lost forever.

10:
Zen and the Art of Putting Down Your Phone

The Internet is amazing if you're using it for gleaning information. We all know what's good about it, you know; where else can I get a gasket for a TEF20 in ten seconds? Or, 'Okay Google, who was Henry Cole?' 'Henry Cole was a washed up TV presenter who had no teeth.' I'm on the Internet to look at the weather and find spare parts and I understand that, but like anything in life that has something incredibly wonderful about it, there is a significant downside.

I really don't understand what is good about social media. That's all downside as far as I can tell. We ain't going to find out for a while just how bad, but it is scarring the youth of today. It's making them totally insecure as far as I can tell. You see, when I was a kid, a teenager, and we weren't invited to a party, we could tell ourselves: 'Oh, he's only got four beds at his house, his mum won't let him have any more people to stay, so that's all right.' Now, they post pictures of the party, in real time, there's forty people having a hooley and you weren't invited. And then perhaps people are commenting, 'Where's Henry?' 'Henry's a knob.' 'He's probably in his shed polishing a brake shoe.' What does that do to long-term psyche when you're exposed to that stuff as a kid? We won't know till it's too late.

If you have any public profile at all, you get your fair share of abuse on the Internet. I've never read any of it and I think anyone who is remotely famous should probably try and have a level of detachment from it. But for kids, it is not so easy. They can really be hurt. And kids see these other kids (or grown-ups) dissing whoever it may be and the abuse rolls downhill, man, and next thing is your kids are getting abused online. I see these kids and all they care about is their likes. They're smoking and drinking at fourteen, because they are so insecure, and although they are posting pictures of it all, the parents refuse to see it. They don't want to believe it's going on. And that's really worrying because if the parents won't say anything, and the kids are getting all their guidance online, well, no one's going to say anything online to them because they don't want to look square, but someone really needs to say, 'Listen, kid, you're heading the wrong way in life.'

I don't think we'll really know what the Internet has done to us for another fifty years. Are we going to become totally obese because we don't have to do anything? Are we going to be totally insular because we don't actually interact with anybody? Will we have zero personal skills when we are actually around other people, because we are so unused to it?

One of the weirdest things, and I see it today with my

kids, they all go out, yeah, and they're all on their phones! Why would you go out and be on your phone? Stay at home, man, save a lot of money. I think there's been a major miscalculation about the advantages of being online as opposed to, say, the inherent advantages of walking along without your nose in a phone, looking around, and actually being aware of what's going on in life.

It all comes back to reality. The Internet is based on fake aspiration and fantasy. 'I want to be like that YouTuber. I want to have the crib that bloke's got.' It doesn't matter how rich you are, or how successful you are, if you're using the Internet for that kind of behaviour, it's going to make you miserable.

But if you're actually looking for information, searching up about this Chopper that you're going to restore, getting some real clues on that, like on Pinterest and things, then that's great. (Although, even then Pinterest is smeared with pictures of girls in G-strings lying all over a Chopper. I'm just like: 'If I want to watch porn, I'll do it. Just get the girl off there, right, because I just want to look at the bikes.')

So it's a funny one because the Internet is great for a shed dweller because he can order parts, he can order sheds, he can order paint, he can even order a bloke to put up his shed – but sheds are diametrically opposed to everything the Internet stands for.

I think most shed dwellers understand that the Internet overall has had a negative effect on humans. I mean, you can communicate, you have your WhatsApp or whatever it's called and you can become a tribe very easily. But the problem is, I think, it breeds guilt, the Internet. It breeds insecurity. It confuses activity with progress. And it is tragic but it's basically how society's going, and all you can really do about it is retire to the shed and drink tea.

This leads naturally to a very important question: do you need a Wi-Fi signal in a shed? I think, perhaps counter-intuitively, yes, you do, because it's a pain in the arse otherwise if you've got to check something, and I probably do spend an hour and a half online every day just to keep stuff organized. I unfortunately do. That is the reality. It's about discipline, isn't it? It's about that discipline of, you know, 'Let's stick the phone on airplane mode for an hour now.'

Often you can't hear the phone in a shed anyway, because you're milling or polishing or on the lathe. What you do in a shed takes you away because of the noise of what you're doing. Under a welding mask, you're very much in your own little world, aren't you? I just feel you know where you are with a shed. You go in it, you turn the heat on, you sit there, you can be spiritually at peace. You try and leave your worries at the door when you go in – and for me a big part of that is to not be incessantly checking my phone.

So while there are some purists out there who don't allow phones in the shed, and I get where they are coming from, I'm not one of them. It's not a comms blackout zone. I actually find it more stressful having no access to my email than having it. I like to know what's going on. If the phone goes off, I want to see what it is, and then I can be spiritually content that it's not important. I can see a message come in and think, 'That doesn't matter right now, I'll sort it later.'

Also, on a purely practical level, you're often on your own in a shed and if something was to go wrong with an angle grinder or you had a coronary, then you need to have some safety net to alert the relevant parties that you're croaking. That's why I suggest bringing a phone into a shed, but have it on silent.

There needs to be a panic button just in case life takes over. But if you find you're just sitting in your shed obsessively checking Snapchat and your bank balance, then maybe try ditching the phone at the door. Because a shed is a place to dwell, to take time, to be away, to take a break from all that rubbish.

11:
The Life-changing Magic of Sheds

I do think that the opportunity for manual endeavour and creativity that a shed provides means that the shed does have a very important spiritual and soul-nurturing purpose. For the average unreconstructed male, especially if you spend a lot of your life behind a computer screen or a steering wheel, there are not that many opportunities to express yourself in daily life.

But your shed is about nothing but expressing yourself. Whether it's restoring those petrol cans you have been collecting all your life (guilty), making a beautiful wooden chair or a one-hour mission to put a new fuel line in your strimmer, working on something or contemplating something in the shed is as close as I'll ever get to meditating and doing yoga and all that other good stuff that the women in my life seem to gravitate towards so easily.

But the other really wonderful thing about a great shed is that when it gets an atmosphere and develops a bit of mojo, it can be a place where men come together. Just last week, I saw a geezer break into song in a shed. Irish Tommy, he's seventy-eight years old, and he turns up at my mate Mick's shed, which is full of random antiques, oil lamps and old Guinness signs on the side of his motor vehicle workshop.

It's a miserable day but this geezer, Tommy, he's full of the joys of spring. He starts telling us how some young lad gave him a pound of CBD butter and he has been putting it on his toast in the morning, then he starts singing this Irish navvies' song about working for McAlpine digging tunnels for the London Underground in the 1960s, 'McAlpine's Fusiliers' it's called. I mean, he is jumping up and down in the air by the end of it and we are all literally falling over laughing.

Now, look, it might be the CBD butter at work, but do you think he would have done that in the house? In the garden? Where a woman might see him? Course he bloody wouldn't. That was shed stuff. Because a shed is the last place where an unreconstructed male can really get in touch with his soulful side. It's also a place where men can come together, with their mates, talk nonsense and get a cup of tea and a biscuit and just chat. Women can talk on the phone all day. But men don't really like picking up the phone. If I see a bloke calling me on the phone, my first reaction is, 'Oh shit, what's happened?'

There is this misconception that men are sitting in their sheds talking shit about their women, but that's rarely the case in my experience. But, if a man is ever going to have a conversation with another man about his prostate gland outside of a doctor's office, I tell you what, a shed is the place.

That, of course, is what the whole Men's Shed movement is about. They have this brilliant slogan, which is 'Men don't talk face to face, they talk shoulder to shoulder.' Too true man. The geezers who go to Men's Sheds call themselves 'Shedders' and there is even a university professor, Barry Golding, who came up with the term 'shedagogy' to describe 'the way some men prefer to learn informally in shed-like spaces mainly with other men.'

Men's Sheds popped up all over Ireland and the UK after the big financial bust of 2007 as communities realized they needed to look after their men. The roots of the Men's Sheds movement goes back to the 1980s in Broken Hill, New South Wales, Australia, where former miners set up sheds as places to meet and get on with a bit of manual work – most of the Men's Sheds have basic woodwork tools, a lathe, a welding kit and art supplies. And a kettle for tea, obviously. They have won loads of awards over the years, including in 2010, a Suicide Prevention Award. That's amazing. So if you're a geezer who's having a hard time, well, guess what? Hanging out in a shed talking rubbish with a few other blokes might actually save your life.

The trouble is, men are in trouble. Sometimes it can seem like there's no hope for us. The only time we have any kind of sympathy from the opposite sex is when we've got a disease. But what is a man's role in this modern world, and what is a woman's role in this modern world? Over centuries the male-female situation has been how it is. And over the last twenty years really, probably less, people have tried to change it. I am fully into equal rights for everyone and equal opportunities for everyone. I'm the first there in the queue. But what is the legacy at the end of the day for the men?

Where does everyone fit in society? I don't understand what I should do. I don't know how to be.

Like, should I open the door for a woman any more or should I let it slam in her face? And if I can't open a door, what functions do we have any more? What are we there for? To protect? Well, people would have a major issue with that right now. Are we there to breed? You can do that with a syringe these days, can't you? So, are we there to earn money? Well, a woman can earn as much as a man.

I've got a friend at the moment whose wife is a professional, and he's a professional and there are issues around that family construct in the sense of who's doing what in the family. This is a *major* issue for people these days. Gone are the days for a lot of family units where the bloke goes, 'Going to work, babe, see you at five.' And the woman's there looking after the kids. I get that it wasn't ideal but it worked more or less for a long old time.

You know, this whole construct of family is evolving and changing before our very eyes. And if we're not careful we're actually going to disenfranchise every element of that family, because we actually really don't know what we want. Women coming of age and doing what they want to do is great. I think we all agree, hopefully, that that's a great thing. But where does that leave us? What is left for a man to do, and what can he do without any guilt that perhaps he's doing something wrong?

Maybe we are there to take the bins out, but I've just seen my wife bringing the bins back in, God bless her, so that's another job whipped from under our noses. I mean, in our family I always drive but Google are on to that too. Moving furniture? Maybe. Are men better cooks? Not in the real world, son. But are we the best at tinkering with stuff in a shed? Definitely. I think that what the Men's Shed movement understands is that sheds are the best way to get to know someone, and safe places to reveal a little of yourself.

To say I wasn't a mad supporter of Jeremy Corbyn would be fair comment, but I read this interview with Corbyn and Theresa May, when they were going head to head in one of the elections, and the interviewer says: 'What do you do, Theresa May, when you're not working?' She goes, 'I go walking with my husband.' Big deal. Then they said, 'Jeremy Corbyn, what do you do?' and he goes, 'Well, my dad used to collect photographs and go and take photographs of manhole covers, Victorian manhole covers, and I like doing that.' And I'm reading this, and I think, 'Hang on a sec, blimey, there's a man with soul. There's a man who actually is interested in our industrial past, which a lot of these people purport to be, just because they want to get elected, but they aren't really. I warmed to Jeremy Corbyn as a human being a bit after that.

And it gave me this great idea: what if you could get the politicians in a shed? You get David Cameron in, you get Jeremy Corbyn in, you get Boris in, you get the tea on. I wouldn't want to talk to them about politics at all. I'm not interested in politics, I'm interested in them as people. I'd want them to bring something into the shed to restore. So, we can restore something together, be it a lamp, be it something to polish, just something small, you don't want to make them look stupid or anything like that, because I think you find out what a person's really like in a shed.

I would call it 'Shed Talk'. I'd want them to go, 'Oh, I'll go and have a cup of tea with Henry and shoot the breeze.' And, you know, we would sort of, hopefully quite cleverly, actually get to the root of what these people are.

You have to do some kind of endeavour with a bloke to find out what they're really like. And that might be trying to fix a wiring issue on my Kawasaki H1 or it might be trying to fix his bicycle or something like that. You see how they take on and approach things, whether they give up very quickly or can't be bothered, or if they get really ratty if it doesn't happen immediately.

Patience and tolerance are two of the greatest virtues in a shed, but then again, you know, the actual psyche that you need to be able to restore something is very relevant to how you are in the real world. If you're smart, you ask for advice and you will listen to advice in the shed. You will let Allen Millyard do whatever he does there to help you rather than thinking that you are being somehow emasculated by him telling you what to do. It's a microcosm of life, a shed, when you're restoring something.

It's all about how you deal with challenges in a shed and the great thing about being in a shed is you can make mistakes, and no one will hear you scream when you realize that there's a few springs left over from that clutch you were restoring after you put the cover on, you know?

Working side by side with another man in a shed does

reveal a man's psyche and a man's character very quickly, without doubt. If you spend a long time in a shed with them you'll know, for example, very quickly that they're very easily distracted or they, you know, they said they're going to be at the shed at nine o'clock and they turn up at eleven, because they are an unreliable sod.

I often quite happily spend an afternoon talking very important nonsense with other men in my shed. Bob turns up, I make some tea and we're in for the afternoon, telling stories about wheeling and dealing and how it used to be.

One of the things I love about this community is, it doesn't matter who you are. I could be the Duke of Marlborough standing there and it's properly classless because it's about passion and love of history and buying and selling. Some of the richest geezers you'll ever meet are shed dwellers, but you wouldn't know it if you met them. Go to an auction and, this is no exaggeration, there are people there in old holey Barbours. I promise you someone will be standing there with bailing twine holding their coat together. And the auctioneer goes, 'Brough Superior, SS100, what am I bid? Shall we start the bidding at a hundred grand?' And they are all bidding away.

A shed is amazing because it allows you to strip away the façade of social pretence, as regards the way you dress, the way you behave, and just reveals you the way you are. A shed allows you to be you, and for you to express you, hence it is quite a private place. It's a place where you only let people in who you trust. Out there, you have to mix with a wide variety of people but in the shed, you're keeping it tight, you're not letting just anyone in, because they could turn out to be a pirate.

I think you need to be of common mind with anyone you allow in your shed. There aren't any airs and graces in a shed. There's no arrogance in a shed. There's no keeping up with the Joneses in a shed and, in my view, that is because a shed is what you are.

So, you have to be very careful who you let into that shed, just as careful as who you'd emotionally let into your deepest inner thoughts, because if someone comes in and disses you in your shed, or disses your latest resto, it might never be the same for you, which would be a tragedy. If you're coming in my shed, this is me laid bare, right? So, consequently I am trusting you to embrace me. I'm bringing you in here to show you my Shell Duo can, but not in a boastful way. I am asking you in because I think you might be interested in it.

But I'm not going to walk down the King's Road with my Shell Duo can under my arm, am I, giving it the massive? But actually, that Shell can says so much more about me than my Aston Martin on hire-purchase. You're going to find the real me if you come into my shed, okay, because the rest of it is bubble-gum packaging to keep up with the Joneses. I don't want a new Range Rover; I don't want one. It doesn't say a thing about me other than that I have an okay credit score.

The thing about shedders is that we understand that there is no sense in buying a modern motorcycle which you just ride off on, when you can buy a vintage motorcycle that you can restore, you can tinker with *and* you can ride.

Come into my shed and you're going to find out how I'm actually organized on the inside, what my real priorities are in life. A shed is the ultimate reflection of my soul. When people I don't know that well are coming round for lunch, I shut the doors and my shed hides. If I like two of the people, then after lunch I might ask them if they want to come and have a look in my shed. But you don't put it on display straightaway.

Here's a classic shed moment: one day Mel turns up, people will know him from the TV shows, and he's telling wonderful stories about buying a Spitfire for sixty quid and another one, about a guy who tried to sell him a Harrier Jump Jet, and it's all that kind of caper. Who would be interested in that? Shed dwellers. Because we're interested in what those things are. And also, what comes from shed dwelling is an innate love of history and our British past.

And to me, what is so exciting about dwelling in a shed, is everyone can get involved; because you're in a shed, you can be trusted. We're all singing from the same potato, aren't we, because we're all shed dwellers and it's a community.

One of our favourite topics of conversation is about the outside world and how it's a nightmare. It is them and us, you know. And just like you've got a bunker at your strategic positions in a war, we have our bunkers of sheds, because out there, it's Armageddon as far as we're concerned, because we see the past as something to embrace, not the future. The future is rubbish. The only reason why we look at the future is to help us think what to buy and put in our sheds that could be worth some money in the future.

Like Mel saying: 'Henry, buy plastic. Bob's got a steam engine in the shed. A full-size steam engine. Unbelievable. He built the shed for the steam engine.'

Yeah, it is a bit unbelievable, but it's also all true. That is what shed dwelling is all about. Come in, have a yarn, maybe buy something, load it up and drive off back to your own shed.

12:
Sheds on TV

One of the main things I want to do in this book is to say a massive thank you to everyone who has ever tuned in and watched one of my TV shows. Thank you, every last one of you, for giving me this life.

Shed and Buried was born out of a dream I had about doing a TV show about sheds presented by people who weren't TV presenters. Now, I know that sounds ridiculous, and yes, I had presented TV shows before, but I don't think anyone could confuse me with Anneka Rice. I mean, I have no teeth to start with. It was a very vague idea to begin with, but what really kicked it into higher gear was that it coincided with me meeting the legend that is Sam Lovegrove.

Sam and I came together on the Bonneville Salt Flats in Utah, and he actually built the bike, the classic Brough Superior, that I did the land speed record on. It was an absolutely wonderful experience and Sam and I instantly hit it off, but I really knew we were going to be mates forever when I was sitting on this bike in full race leathers in the boiling hot weather at the starting line with Sam and a couple of other mechanics around, and I said to Sammy, 'Give me some advice, mate.' And he goes, 'Just imagine you're going to the shops to get some jelly babies.' I say,

'What do you mean by that?' He says, 'You're just going down the shops for some jelly babies, okay?' What a legend, and exactly what I had come to expect of our Sam.

When we were preparing for that trip, I went down to his place, and he invited me into his shed. It was everything that you'd expect, everything that you could ever want; the ultimate shed. It soon became quite obvious that he was not only a demon bike builder, but also a proper shed dweller. He is a bit of a hippy, so I wasn't surprised to see a coal-fired burner which he had built himself in his shed to keep it warm. His shed is stone built and I was struck by the beautiful sense of orderly disorder which you get in working sheds. There were tools laid out everywhere, but all the work surfaces were mint. All the things he was working on were laid out perfectly. There was this great smell of metal that's been chafed, and there was this sense that the whole place was not only a product of hard work and passion but a place where hard work and passion could be unleashed.

He spends his whole life in the shed; his house really is just, well, it's just a place to go to the lavvy, to be honest. That's its purpose. Sam is a very dark horse and what you might not realize from watching him arse about with me in the van is that he is a genius. I mean, really; from 1998 to 2001 he spent his time running a team of thirty people designing one of the first hydrogen fuel cells. He was chief of design and development at a company that designed hydrogen fuel cells which will eventually power taxis and buses when people realize what a load of cobblers trying to do it on batteries is. He was flying on planes all around the world doing this, designing cutting-edge technology but he did what everyone dreams of doing and hasn't got the balls to do – he chucked in the 100 grand a year job to follow his passion: pre-war cars and motorcycles.

He is, without question, the world leader on Brough Superior restoration. People are begging him to take on their £100,000–£500,000 motorcycles. Jay Leno relies on him for his restos. At the moment he's got a very wealthy client who sent him a frame and half a Brough SS100 engine. Sam has recreated and milled out the other half of the engine. *He's made the other half of the engine.* The cases, everything. And you can't tell what's the new bit and what's the old one. That's genius.

As the instigator and co-creator of one of the most incredible moments of my life, which was doing that land speed record at Bonneville, I came to trust him completely. For instance, the bike had a rev counter, but no speedo. One of my main jobs, as the pilot, was to watch the rev counter absolutely meticulously, because Sam had told me to keep it at 4,600. And because I trusted him so completely, I didn't do 4,650, or 4,575. I did 4,600 revs and the bike did what he said it would.

And to share with somebody the pain, the anguish, the excitement and the self-doubt that you have lying on a bike before you launch it at the Bonneville Salt Flats is a great starter to a relationship. We just got on so well on the salt, and we shared so many interests and fascinations, that we immediately bonded. To be honest, it's very difficult at my age to make new friends, proper friends. Most of my friends are from school or from motorcycling in the early days. And to find someone who was so like-minded in one way, but obviously so completely not like-minded in others – you know, the guy's a bean-eating hippy and I'm the furthest away from that you can possibly be – was amazing and our relationship burgeoned.

I knew he would be great on telly, and so right after he said the thing about the jelly babies, I said to him, 'Mate, if I survive, do you fancy doing a show where you and I go into sheds and drink tea?' And then this dude standing beside me with a massive green flag gives it a wave and says, 'God speed,' and that's my cue to go, and as I sped off, Sammy shouted after me: 'Yeah, all right.'

That was the start and we didn't know what to call it. It was originally going to be called *Dead in the Shed*, but we went to the broadcaster and they said, 'That's a bit morbid,' and I said, 'Well, that's the fun of it, isn't it?' They didn't see the joke really. The credit has to go to Hamish, my managing director, who rang up one Sunday and said, 'How about *Shed and Buried*?' I said, 'Bloody hell, that's amazing, how did you think of that?' He goes, 'I don't know, it's quite unusual.' I went, 'Unusual? I've never heard you say anything decently creative in your life, mate, it's a ruddy miracle.'

What I really love about the name is that it captures the potential dark side of being a shedder. There's lots of people who've buried stuff in the shed, but they've buried it too far and they have become hoarders rather than collectors.

It is frustrating when you go into a shed and see incredible pieces of our automotive history rusted through, but I do have compassion for these people, because I'm a bit of a hoarder myself and I firmly believe that collecting is an expression of addiction. I am addicted to collecting, but I try and keep it in check. How many petrol pumps have I got? Ten. How many oil dispensers? Five. I don't need an intervention quite yet.

But the guys with the barns full of rusting cars? I think they need people in, but usually, you can't reach them. Some of them just flatly refuse to let us in. I think it is because they feel so guilty that they have destroyed so many vehicles. Deep down, they feel awful that they've done that. I'm convinced that people have that issue. Sometimes people go, 'I've got to put my hands up, Henry. I bought this to restore it and I ain't got the time. So you can have it for half what I paid for it.' Those are the people who are catching it early. They're doing the right thing. They're taking a hit while it can still be salvaged, before the metaphorical (or literal) frame has rusted through.

So, basically *Shed and Buried* was born thanks to Hamish and Sam, and we sat down and we had a corporate meeting with the suits. Hamish is brilliant at these things; he gets a soy latte on, and talks it all up big time, but, as much as he tossed the whole thing around, the reality was that me and Sam were just going to let our facial hair run wild, drive around, go into some sheds, find some things to buy and try and fix them up and sell them. That's all it ever was and all it ever will be, because, basically, that's what I want to watch. I don't want to have any convoluted format and all that kind of stuff. I just want it straight up, 'Hello, welcome to the show, here's me and Sammy on our voyage of discovery to Sussex. We're going to a great shed where there are lots of motorbikes, right, Sammy?' 'Yeah, let's get there and have a rummage about Henry.' Then we get there, buy a bike, go home, do it up and flog it. And because we kept to that simple mantra, and ITV allowed us to do that, the show got fans.

It appeals to shed dwellers but also people who like the idea of being shed dwellers one day, and who, instead of going to Alton Towers for the day, or going to see *Cats* in the West End, would really rather go and see someone else's shed, and see if we may be able to buy a Puch Maxi off him. Sammy and I don't really want to go to some posh London restaurant, you see, we would much rather be stopping at a Little Chef (or whatever they're called now), and that's why it works. And so, Sam's come with me on this journey over the last six years. We spend our days sitting on the back of steam traction engines trundling through the British countryside. You can't get better than that. And that's called *work*, by the way.

There's been relationships in my life where I've thought, 'Oh I really would like to continue a relationship with that person,' but I end up not doing it for different reasons. But you only meet a certain number of these people in your life, and, as you get older, you realize, when you do meet them, you must do everything in your power to hang on to them. Sheds give you the ability to be able to do that because it's something you can do together. Thank God I did that with Sam, I really gave it a proper go and he's become my best mate. I think it's pretty clear that our friendship is genuine.

We don't give a toss what we say on telly. We don't give a toss that the camera's rolling. If we open a shed and there's a rust bucket in there, we will say so. If we open the shed and there's a Norton Inter in the corner, we will both go mad. And also, we have that relationship whereby we know whatever we say to each other is for love rather than one-upmanship. We're just genuine blokes who like each other who are much more interested in the subject matter than our position on that subject matter. I don't give a monkey's whether Sammy's doing an interview or I'm doing it, if he's riding the bike or I'm riding it. It's never even crossed either of our minds.

I think there are other people out there on telly who have that relationship like we do, like the Hairy Bikers. You can tell with those two lads that they're genuine. But you can't organize that. You can't make that happen. It's got to come from the heart. Everything that Sammy and I do does genuinely come from the heart. I think that we're aspirational in a non-aspirational way, by which I mean we're not flying off to the Luxor in Vegas and snorting cocaine, we're just in a shed, man, because that's where we want to be and people look at us and think, 'Yeah, man, that looks like a laugh.'

I know people who have kept pigs because they were making a TV show about keeping pigs, but once the show was over and the pigs had got the bullet and they had made the final episode about eating Squeaky and Squawky ham sandwiches, they never looked at another pig again. That's just not the case with me and sheds. Absolutely fundamentally not the case.

Long before I got into all of this professionally, I yearned and yearned to have my own shed. Twenty-five years ago, when I was living in London, I dreamt of having something like this. I was living in a tiny little house with no garage, and I had two Lamborghini Countachs, a Porsche 911, a Ferrari 328 GTS and a Harley. I was a flash idiot. I couldn't afford any of them; they were all on tick apart from the Harley. And because I didn't have a shed or a garage to keep them in, I never saw them. I had them all in storage. I never drove them, I never hung out with them, I never chatted to them. I just read *Classic & Sports Car* magazine and dreamt of actually having a shed to put those cars in and to buy more (I told you I was a flash git). But because I was in London, I couldn't do it.

Eventually I decided that, whatever it cost, I would try and create a shed in the middle of London, to at least get the Ferrari under cover, if nothing else. So, I sold my soul and bought an even tinier house, right, but it had a garage. Emotionally I was fully invested. I thought it was going to be great but when I actually got the keys and drove it over there I was totally distraught because I could get a Ferrari in there and the Harley, but I still couldn't look at them because the garage was so small that I couldn't be in there with them. I had to push the Ferrari in, because I couldn't get out of it once it was in. I couldn't even crawl through the window.

So, what did I do? Much as I thought that I wanted a place to stash my car, I actually ended up putting all the cars in storage again, and that was a defining moment. Because, I could have the Harley in my little garage, right, *and* I could have a workbench, and when I wasn't tinkering with the Harley, I was building remote control helicopters.

I was also trying to work out how I could continue my passion for model railways. I put it on a pulley system coming down from the ceiling. So while I thought I wanted a shed or garage to store my beautiful cars and bikes, the real benefit I was getting from a shed was actually to be in there, creating something. Who gives a monkey's if Henry Cole has created a remote control helicopter? I do. No one else does. You try showing it to my wife. Eventually, I sold the two Countachs for seventy-five and eighty-five grand respectively. They'd both be worth half a million quid now. So, if I'd actually moved out to the country, and had the shed that I always dreamt of, I'd be a millionaire. That still guts me.

When we finally moved to the country twenty years ago and I started to be able to have sheds, that's when the realization of it being an integral part of my psyche and my life took hold. And so consequently, I'm trying to say that the reason why those TV shows work is because they are authentic. Like all good factual TV shows, they're born out of a real passion, and the reason why I bust my arse trying to get motorcycles and shed dwelling on telly, is because that is my life, my passion. The passion came before the show and it will be there afterwards.

The only problem I can foresee when it ends is that I won't get into such decent quality sheds, because I'm not doing it for telly, or I won't be able to buy the stuff that I can buy now because I won't get access to it, do you see what I mean? So, that is the real situation. My shed love is real.

When I came up with the show *Shed and Buried,* I told Channel 4 it was a flog-it style TV show about fixing up old junk. It's actually about shed dwellers, and the complicated relationship men (it's nearly always men) have with their sheds. Most of us believe our sheds are sacred, and so is everything in them. In my case that means the spider in the corner is not to be disturbed, nor are the blue tits nesting under the eaves, or the community of ladybirds that live under a 1950s hessian sack.

That's why there is usually an interview process before you are allowed in a geezer's shed. When Sam and I turn up at a new place for *Shed and Buried,* we go into the kitchen and meet the wife first. We're in their house with our shoes off, drinking tea, so they can see if we're all right to go in the shed. I get it. Letting someone into your shed is like being stripped naked. When I let someone in, I am baring my soul to them.

A shed is about being in touch with yourself. And that's what most of us, whether we admit it or not, strive for all our lives: to try and understand *who we are.* And actually, with a bit of time, on your own, in your shed, you can find out.

My utopia...

Everything good in this world was created in a shed.

Before Paul the shed surgeon got to work...

...and after Paul had worked his magic.

Don't knock it down: save it!

Even my office is a shed...

Left: Even if it's tiny, love it, and accessorise.

Below: Some flora never goes amiss on a shed.

Above: Shed seating is vital.

Left: Cubby-hole shelving is an absolute must.

Vintage signs: the perfect shed wall adornment.

A shed and a model railway: double escapism.

Left: Sammy's quilted boiler suit changed my life.

Below: Allen Millyard built this in his tiny shed!

Left: Si, my upcycling fellow TV shed dweller.

Below: The ultimate shed companions: Sammy and Jellybean.

I love it when I am walking down the street and people stop me because I think the way you really show your appreciation to your fans is to give them five minutes of your time. When I get stopped in the street, and the person says, 'Henry, mate, I love your shows,' I go, 'Have you got a shed?' 'I have actually, mate. I collect vintage horse tack and antique saddles.' 'Do you mate?' I say. 'What have you picked up lately? Where do you go for that kind of stuff?' There's immediately that relationship because although I'm the guy on the telly and he is the guy who is watching at home on the sofa (or in the shed) with a cup of tea, we're both shed dwellers, we've got that in common, so we've got the basis for a conversation.

There's a reason for people to come up and talk to me, and there's also a fascination for me in finding out what they are into (as well as a bit of a vested interest because, hey man, they might have the long-lost Harley headlight that I really want to buy, do you know what I mean?).

The shed audience comes up to me the whole time. I know them well. *Find It, Fix It, Flog It* is a very different audience and different kind of people and I don't get many people wanting to chat about it. It's a daytime audience: people on shift work, mums, carers and students, I think maybe they are a bit too cool for school to come up to me.

I guess my part on *Flog It* . . . is to be the eccentric. This bloke who lives in a shed and is covered in oil the whole time. I'm the foil for Simon O'Brien, basically. Simon's all about the future. He's all about upcycling. He's all about changing the use of something. He's all about mullering something to make it worth more, and what I'm about is restoration. Retaining British heritage. Making something look more beautiful *without* mullering it.

A lot of the work in *Flog It . . .* is cleaning: you're just taking off all the decay and rust and then you lacquer it or polish it. Like, we got a forklift in one of the shows. It was just languishing in a shed, it was absolutely destroyed. It may look destroyed still, but it now works mint. And all we did was clean it, got it going, sorted out the hydraulics and the air lines and rattle-canned the wheels black. I've got fifteen cans of Caterpillar yellow in the shed now, because we were going to re-spray it but actually we decided at the last minute not to repaint the bodywork because we kind of like the smashed up look which it has. But the real point is that it now works brilliantly. If it didn't work, and looked smashed-up, then it's useless. But if it looks smashed up and works like a gem, which it does, it's phenomenal.

Shed and Buried was such a joyous thing that we wanted to do more of it, so when we got a call from Channel 4 saying they wanted to do something similar but that 'had an element of upcycling to it,' I said, 'Great, but I don't even know how to spell "upcycling", so you're going to have to get someone else to work with me.' And so anyway, through a long and convoluted sequence of events, Simon turned up. He used to be in *Brookside* did our Si, and his hobby and his profession is buying houses which don't have any roofs on and sorting them out.

People like it; we've done over 130 one-hour shows of it. I restore, he upcycles and at the end of each show they value how much each of those items is worth and we pay the people, the shed dweller, that money for their item. I think *Find It, Fix It, Flog It* has proved a great success for daytime audiences because it mixes light shedding with styling. It's *Shed and Buried* lite, that's what it is, for your armchair shedder.

We don't get into the detail of what that stationary engine is and its history and all that kind of thing, mainly because it's a daytime audience who just want to see a terrible stationary engine covered in mud and oil become a beautiful gleaming one, and quite rightly so. They don't need the rest of it.

I have this theory about *Shed and Buried* and *Find It, Fix It, Flog It* which is that, while on the surface those shows are about restoration and transformation, they are really both about conversation. It's about the banter that Simon and I have in the shed, it's about the banter that I have with Millyard when we're restoring and that Si has with Gemma and Phil when they're upcycling.

It's all about conviviality. And that's what a shed, and being in a shed, should be about. You know, you really don't want to go and get depressed in a shed, yeah? Go and get depressed somewhere else like a bedroom or a lavatory. But getting depressed is something that you shouldn't be doing in a shed. That should be your divine intervention. Your little light at the end of a very long day, and that is also about conversation. And it's about taking the mickey a bit, and it's about having fun with your mate.

Simon's not a shedder. He lives in a town, and he's got no shed to stash stuff in, so he has very little interest in acquiring stuff. But for Sam and I, that's pivotal. We're massively about whether we can actually relieve the shed dweller of the item for the right price. That is critical to any shed dweller.

So, thank you so much to those of you watching my shows; it means I get to carry on doing this. You guys watching my shows means I don't have to do a proper job, if you see what I mean. I can just immerse myself in my passion. I don't have to work on a factory floor, or be middle management at an insurance company, or sell vegetables.

I did once get a job as a security guard in Selfridges and it didn't turn out too well. A mate of mine – we must have been about nineteen, and it was Christmas – he goes, 'Do you want some extra money?' I went, 'Yeah, what have you got, man?' He goes, 'They're looking for security guards in Selfridges.' I went, 'Really, are they?' So, I applied, not online, you had to go in in those days and I filled out the form. And they rang me and said come in for an interview, so I went in and got the job. And they said, 'Right, start Monday.' I went, 'All right.'

So, I turn up and I go, 'Right, just give us a walkie-talkie, I'll be there. Or shall I go undercover?' And this supervisor guy, he goes, 'Well, you can't really do that, Henry.' I went,

'Okay, look, all right, if you give me a uniform I'll do it like that, where's the uniform, do I get measured up?' 'No, it's not quite like that, Henry.' 'What do you mean by that?' I say. He goes, 'Oh, well you've got two weeks' training.' 'But it'll be Christmas by then,' I say. And he goes, 'Would you come with me?'

So, I walked down this corridor, into this room. There are twenty people in there, in white sleeveless shirts with product in their hair, and I just knew I could never work there. I couldn't do it. I said: 'Nah, you're all right. I'm off. Something's popped up.' They even gave me my tube fare back home, I seem to recall. I just remember thinking, 'Why do I have to train? I can spot dodgy people. I'm a dodgy geezer myself. I can see a knobhead nicking stuff.' But no, companies in general want you to train, and conform, and be like them, and put product in your hair and I just refuse to do that.

The only other job I ever had was scamming people into getting haircuts so I am probably being deeply hypocritical when I say I can't abide the charity guys on the street, the chuggers. 'Hello, can I just have a word with you, mate? Hello, mate. Mate, mate, mate, mate.' There is an army of them down the street. Five of them and you're just trying to get to Argos. I would say they mean well, but I worry that a lot of them don't, because I used to do it with leaflets for this hairdresser's on the King's Road called Scissors.

'Hello mate, eh, do you want a free consultation upstairs, yeah, about your hair? Here, have a leaflet, we've got . . .' and I'd make it up, 'Fifty per cent off today, yeah? All right. Can

I take you up?' 'All right,' they'd say. 'Great. There you go. Sharon, here's someone who needs a free consultation.' And another quid to me. Nice. 'Hello mate, fancy a consultation?'

At least that was honest commerce, it's when charity becomes commercial, and people are earning commissions off it, then it upsets me, because I don't know where my money's going. I think there's probably better ways of collecting for charity, you know? But it's not celebrities doing Pudsey. If you said to those celebrities, 'You're going to ride a bicycle from Land's End to John O'Groats, but you're not allowed to tell anyone about it, ever, but you'll make a million quid for charity,' very few of them would do it. That's quite upsetting, innit?

I've actually been with people when they're having those conversations and it's like, 'Well, this year, mental health is a good thing to support, it shows that you're very vulnerable and, you know, suicide prevention's a bit last year. So shall we do mental health? I mean Harry and William are doing it.' 'Yeah, I might get a dinner with William. You never know.' It's so cynical and perhaps I'm cynical to even suggest it, but that's what I hope my shows are: the antidote to cynicism.

We don't do cynical. We're just there having a giggle. Why would there be cynicism in a shed? It goes back to this whole thing of authenticity. Shed dwelling is about you. It's not about the extension of you. If you're going to enjoy or immerse yourself in shed dwelling, it's got to be for you and nobody else. I just hate anything in this world that seeks to manufacture emotions, and I hate how people are so gullible.

I went to an ITV thing the other day, a talent party. Sammy and I went just to gawp at a few celebs. It was at the Royal Festival Hall and on our tickets, it said, 'Your red carpet time is 6:05.' Now that immediately says a lot about how they see you. The meat and potatoes are coming in at 7:15, the doors are shut at 7:30 and the really famous people are coming at 7:35 when the doors are closed. Me and Sammy are 6:05 folk.

Normally I would just not be there, right, but I say, 'All right, Sammy, you and me, mate, we'll go along for a giggle.' So, we turn up and this woman goes, 'Oh, you want to go down that line please.' So I went, 'All right, come on, Sam.' Well, that line was the tradesman's entrance. She thought, quite understandably, because we had just come out of a shed, and looked like it, that we were probably delivering some glasses or something.

So, we go down this line, right, and all the photographers – well, not all of them but about eight of them – go, 'Henry, mate, hello son. I love your shows. Hello Sammy.' They don't take photos; they just chat with us about our shows because they know that me and Sammy ain't going to make it into *Hello!* We're not *Daily Mail* showbiz pages are we? We're not going to be on *I'm a Celebrity* . . . and we know it.

So, Sammy and I go through, right, and then we go up to this balcony to get a drink because we're like literally the first there, and we look out of this window and all the *Love Island* contestants are turning up at 6:32. They've all got their tits out, they're all giving it large with the side boob. They're all checking their make-up, they're all being flashed like crazy and people the next day are going to go, 'Oh Amy's nipple's sticking out. Nice.'

So we go into the Royal Festival Hall and I suddenly realize that the whole point of this thing is for ITV to promote themselves to all the marketing people from M&S and Waitrose. Everyone who advertises on ITV is there. The guys who pay for it all are meeting the stars, schmoozing, all that kind of thing.

Olly Murs and Tom Jones are singing, showcasing some new show. Now, I take a look at who is sitting where. It's all very glamorous. Row one: Phillip Schofield, Holly Willoughby, Paddy McGuinness, Keith Lemon, Piers Morgan. Row two: Jonathan Ross. Hmm? Is he on the way out? Davina McCall in row two. Is *she* on the way out? I don't know. But you can tell first row, all smug. Second row, hmm. Not so smug. Third row: all the *Good Morning Britain* presenters. And they seem pretty happy with that because they might still be heading towards the front row, one day. Fourth row *Love Island* contestants. All of them, and they're pretty happy with that, I think, because they know damn well next year they won't be in a row. Row five? Ainsley Harriott, Henry Cole, Sam Lovegrove.

When we came out of the gig, everyone was going off for a party and Sammy and I were thinking we'd had enough and would clear off now, and maybe go for a pizza. When we came out, all the lads were putting the barriers away. Stacking them on the lorry, and they go, 'All right, Henry, Sam, come on over. Let's have a pic.'

That just summed it up for me. All them lot understand how important a shed, or the love of something that you're passionate about, which just happens to be automotive, is. All those people in row four, they ain't got a clue. I'm very happy being in row five. I'd be very, very scared if they said, 'Henry, could you . . . do you want to be in row one?' That's the beginning of the end.

I just love the idea that people enjoy what I do. It's an affirmation that what I am doing means something, that we are actually resonating with people and we are entertaining people. Of course, it's great if people can have some takeout and understanding from watching, but I do understand that a lot of the people who watch the shows are armchair restorers, and that's great. They won't be going near a rusty motorcycle. They're not going to try it, are they? They're just going to look at it.

But, you know, how many people do Gordon Ramsay's coq au vin with a vol-au-vent up its arse? No one, but everyone watches cooking shows because they might get a little tip about how to do their toast, or decide to put a bit of cheese in their baked beans. Well, that's why I watch cooking shows anyway. I've never cooked anything in my life (apart from the books) and I think we, in the same way, engender a loose feeling of, 'I'd maybe like to go to an auto jumble one day,' but more importantly it's a window into another world.

Now, there are people who watch our shows and do end up in a shed or at an auto jumble, and that is incredibly special to me because honestly, it changes their lives, but the point is you don't actually have to follow through or else there would only be about 826 people watching each show.

I won't deny good ratings make me feel good and bad ratings make me feel bad; I'm as egotistical as the next idiot.

But I do also know that on the day the ratings collapse and the phone stops ringing (and believe me, it's a case of when not if in this business), I'll keep doing this. Without question. I'd keep hanging out in sheds and I'll wheel and deal because although I'm one of the very few who have managed to make it into a job, it's also much more than that. It's more than a passion. It's a way of life, I guess. It's just what I do.

So, when we have a bad week, and the shows don't do well, or something didn't work, or the show just wasn't as good as it could have been, I am so lucky that I have a place to go. I go to my shed and console myself by stripping out a head gasket. Yes, I do talk to my wife, but she's bored witless of it. So, I come to terms with those kind of issues of low self-worth that the entertainment business sometimes foists on you by retreating to my little world, which is a shed, and I'll shut the door and polish an oil can, and suddenly, all that rubbish goes away, and I am lost in it. Lost in the smell, lost in the activity, lost in the endeavour, like shedders everywhere.

13:
Autojumbles Ain't About the Money (That'll Be Twenty Quid Son)

Somebody said to me the other day, 'What's *Junk & Disorderly* about?' I'll tell you what *Junk & Disorderly* is all about. It's about two old geezers having a laugh. It's about trying to figure out what bike that random headlamp is from. It's about how automotive history makes the world a better place. It's about the joy of being a bloke with oily fingers. It's about me and Sammy immersing ourselves in our passion, which is the vehicular heritage of this great country. It's about normal people doing slightly wacky stuff, but it's wacky stuff that is available to anyone with the passion and the inclination to get in their car and drive down to the Driffield auto jumble.

One thing it's not about is money, which is hugely ironic, given that the whole show is structured around me and Sammy buying stuff and trying to sell it for a profit. *Junk* . . . is literally all about us wheeling and dealing; we are at an auction, buying something. We then go to a shed and buy something else, right, and then we go to an auto jumble and we sell all our wares. So, it is shedding in its purest form. In the whole of the last series, I think we made five grand at ten auto jumbles, having invested probably fifteen grand, and we've still got some leftovers like a Harley and a few other bits and bobs.

I think the reason why people like *Junk & Disorderly* is not because it shows you how to get rich but because it is an expression of true, real passion. I'll often spend a morning wheeling and dealing, not on telly, because that's what I love to do, and we're taking the fun of that transactional element out of the shed and into the auto jumbles. Of course, the thought that you might actually strike gold one day lingers in the dark corners of every auto jumbler's mind.

So, we may go to an auto jumble, and I still feel this, and I know Sammy does, you go to an auto jumble, you come out of your shed and you're looking around for stuff to put in your shed, but you're thinking, 'I wonder if there's a JAP V-twin engine? There just might be here,' right, or 'Is today the day I find another Victory petrol can, a two-gallon pyramid can that no one knows about?' And yes! There it is. Maybe I might be able to wipe off the grease and see those initials, 'VRC'. No sense wiping the grease off here. Don't want to act too keen. 'How much do you want for this, mate? Twenty quid, son? Right, yeah, I'll take it.'

The other day we left the stall at Newark for a few minutes to get something to eat and it was someone else's lucky day. We left Uncle Graham, who moves all our stuff about, in charge of the stall. And I go, 'All the cans are twenty quid,

Graham, apart from that one, that's one twenty. Right?' So, we go off, we come back, and he goes, 'I think I've done something wrong.' And I go, 'What was that, Graham?' He goes, 'You know you wanted one twenty for that can? Well I got you one twenty . . . quid note.' You what!? I mean, you've got to laugh. We bought that can for ninety quid, we wanted hundred and twenty for it. We cleaned it up, and he sells it for twenty quid.

So, there's a guy (or perhaps a girl, but probably a guy) who's got out of his scratcher and off his arse and come up to Newark, and he has seen that Agri pyramid can with the beautiful images of the tractors on it and gone, 'Wow, that's lovely. I wonder how much he wants for that.' 'Oh, twenty quid, son.' 'Twenty quid? All right. Yeah. I'm not going to argue with that,' or he might have tried to get it down to fifteen and Graham might have held what he thought was his own. He's got a hundred and twenty quid can. He's gone home well happy in the motor, going, 'You'll never believe it; I got this for twenty quid,' do you know what I mean? That's his week made.

I think *Junk & Disorderly* taps into this good-heartedness at the core of the resto/auto jumble community. It's two old blokes, right, me and Sammy, genuinely going about our business with a total and utter passion for wheeling and dealing old things. And you know what, when we are in that world we don't give a damn about anything else.

And while it's not about the money, per se, that totting up process at the end is great. It's a bit of a laugh. If it doesn't add up we allow ourselves to say, 'Well, we can put that into next week,' because that's what passion is about. There have been thousand quid days, but we have also had eight quid days and twenty-three quid days and I think people really connect to those days, those days that are absolutely ridiculous when it comes to profit and loss but are still a great laugh.

One side note is that while it's not about the money, it definitely is about the transactions. The human contact, the keeping the stock moving, keeping the wheels turning, finding stuff, trading stuff, making deals, shaking hands and hoping the guy really is going to come back with the money.

That excitement of what you might be able to find is exactly what is missing from the British high street today. The reason why the high street is in so much trouble is because it's all the same and no one working at those places is even allowed to talk to you. There's nothing to discover on the high street. You walk down the street and there's Costa. It's worth a latte, and we know exactly what it's going to taste like, and that's fine. Then you have M&S, Next, H&M, it's all the same. It's not an event. It's totally predictable. The high street is a load of rubbish and I feel sad about the way it's gone for my kids, to be honest.

I used to ride my motorbike down the King's Road in the eighties (I once crashed into a bollard outside Blush's restaurant because I was trying to impress a bird on my DT400 and didn't see the bollard) and the King's Road, like Carnaby Street, was something else. There were shops that you'd never seen before, there were clothes that you'd never seen before, there were people dressed like you'd never seen before. It was mind blowing. Now, you ride down the King's Road, it's all the same. All the high street stores are there. It's bleak, it's boring, it's predictable. It's Starbucks, it's Claire's, it's Costa Coffee and the bottom line is that every high street in every big town now is the same. There is no individuality about it.

But there is an oasis in various small towns which, if you are a potential shed dweller, you must make it your business to congregate at, which is your ironmonger's or hardware store. I'm talking about our old traditional ironmonger's, like there's one called Wainwright's in Lechlade that people from my area will know, and you go in there and that is basically a retail shed.

If you are even thinking about getting a shed, if the pangs of shed envy are coming on, the first thing to do is go into your local hardware store, stand at the counter for a bit, smell it, feel it, and just soak up where that shop comes from in our heritage and in our history. And if that makes you feel good, you have to get a shed. It's like how you go and try out a few leather jackets before you buy one.

The ironmonger's is, I think, still a place where a community can come together and discuss the relative merits of buying steel versus zinc-tipped nails, the advantages of Gorilla Glue over Loctite and the adaptability of Tec7 versus your basic silicon.

There's another fantastic hardware store in the town near me and I think it's probably been there for a hundred years. I bought a door handle and latch for my house there thirteen years ago, and after thirteen years the little catch snapped off just by being slammed by kids twenty times a day or what have you. I went back to the ironmonger's with the little bit of fitting and I was like, 'Could you fix this for me? I bought it here.'

Then we all stood around and had a look at it. Tommy, one of the geezers who works there, suggested soldering the two pieces back together but John was like, 'Nah, it just won't have the strength because it's cast iron, if you try and weld it, it just won't be strong enough.' Then Tommy, who's got this mad wiry black curly hair spilling out of a flat cap, says: 'I'll get in touch with that manufacturer and get another one of those pieces. Leave it with me.'

Yeah, right. Leave it with me my arse. Well, guess what? Tommy actually followed through. He rang the manufacturer, who was in Coventry or something, and two weeks later Tommy called me. They had got another one of those pieces sent out. So, rather than having to change the whole door handle, I just had to change that little catch. Took about forty seconds.

It shouldn't be amazing to get that call, because there was a time, not long ago, when people bothered to do stuff like that, to treat their customers like human beings, to try and help them, it was just the norm, but it isn't nowadays. It's incumbent on all shed dwellers to use those local hardware stores and never darken the doors of B&Q, or one day you'll wake up and they'll all be gone.

Hardware stores are places where the community of shedders gather, and I guarantee you whenever I go in there with a problem I don't know how to fix, someone will offer me some advice. Like I went in there the other day because our dishwasher isn't draining properly, because the water can't get up the pipe and back down into the drain, because the pump in it is too weak. So it's got to go straight into the pipe at a lower level, and I went in there and I was like, 'Listen, I've got to get this pipe connected into that pipe, how do I do it?'

And Tommy spent, I would say, nine to twelve minutes talking about it, showing me the different bits of pipe and showing me how you connect them. He sold me the cheapest hacksaw that would work, I think it was three quid, and rather than making me buy a whole pot of the glue that you need to stick the pipe together, Tommy asked one of the lads who does a bit of plumbing on the side if he could give me a bit, and this fella scooped some of the goo out of a tub he had in his Jeep and put it in a plastic bag for me. He explained to me how you do it. I got home and I did it. And it works. It cost me twelve quid and it gave me such a buzz.

There's no way I could have done that job without Tommy spending a bit of time explaining it to me. So, for shed dwellers, hardware stores are an amazing resource. They're like the library, where you can go, and you can consult the reference books, it's just that the reference books are humans.

I love the cubbyhole shelving in an old fashioned hardware store; they often have a whole wall of it, with your quarter-inch bolts, your half-inch pipe, your three-quarter inch plugs, your eyes, your threaded bar, your male parts, your female parts. It just really upsets me that the big chains are coming after them. Why? Why does everyone have to put everyone out of business? Why does everyone have to try and rinse everybody on the planet, every day of the week? We must value and support our local community shops. What we must do as shed dwellers is understand that there is a requirement for us to go out and use these shops, especially now as they are struggling so badly, and immerse ourselves in their atmosphere because there is so much expertise and knowledge there.

It's not a one-way street; it's not like, 'Oh, I'm just going to go down to the ironmonger's because I want to give him some money, the poor sod.' It's not that at all. It's just that you only get out of life what you put into it. And if you go down the ironmonger's and you hang out, you will learn stuff from them and then one day someone else will come in asking daft questions and you'll be able to go: 'Actually mate, you could just use a little bit of hosepipe to insulate your poultry netting.'

I think the problem with all those bland high street outfits is that they've given up on providing a service and just want to sell you stuff. Service and wisdom thrown in used to be part of the deal, now it's so rare and it is something to embrace and something which we mustn't let go of, otherwise we're just going to be left with Amazon and a hope and a prayer which in this throwaway society is unlikely to be answered.

The only things that really seem to work on the high street now are foodie places – your farm shop, your delicatessen, your trendy avocado-eating café – because they have a bit of emotion and creativity behind them, and they may actually not treat you like a number, and you might get a pleasant surprise – and that's what auto jumbles have too. You never know what you're going to find.

Like, one time I was at an auto jumble and I bought what's called a 'Governor Clock' from the Triumph factory. They had this huge clock – it says Triumph underneath it, it's about the size of a dustbin lid – and it would have been bolted on the wall of a factory. It's called a Governor Clock, because it's the main clock, and you can run loads of other clocks from it at the same time all round the factory. I mean, I don't need all the governing stuff, as I have no desire to have a centralized time system running to all the different sheds, although we'd have quite a lot fun with that: wind them all forward, and it could have a date as well, so when you come in it goes to 1956 which would suit me down to the ground. But I digress ...

The point is, you never know what's going to happen at the jumble. You never know what's there. Could be anything. Could be your wildest dream, could be a bag of ... stuff. It's normally stuff. But that's okay. When it comes to auto jumbles and shed rummaging, the RRP is really just there as an ice-breaker. You go to a jumble and if you are a jumbler, you've got a motorbike that you want 500 quid for so you're going to put it on at 800. Now, any geezer who turns up and says, 'Yeah, I'll take it for 800,' ain't a jumbler. What you need to do is, you need to start hustling. And when you are an experienced jumbler, you both know exactly where you're going to end up.

There was one geezer the other day who wanted one of our beautiful Dunlop tin signs. He said, 'How much is that?' I went, '200 quid.' He goes, 'No, mate. I can't do that.' Anyway, we settled on 135. Would you believe, weirdly, that he takes out of his pocket 135 quid. Already counted. So, he was way ahead of me. He knew that's what he was going to go to. Not 140, because he didn't have that, 135 was his top whack. If he'd got it for less, that would have been a bit difficult, you know, taking a fiver or tenner off, but he got it for exactly what he thought he was going to pay for it.

With motorbikes and the big stuff it's always a bit more tense. I go, 'It's 800, mate.' There's always an intake of breath at this point, right, followed by a quietness, right, where the guy's thinking, 'How far can I take this with Henry? This is on telly, so I'll probably get away with murder, right?' So, he goes, '400.' And I go, 'Ah, mate, please, nah. 700.' Right. And then he'll go, '700, I can't, mate. The wife'll kill me.' That's always a belter. So, the fun of it is coming to the 500 quid we all knew we were going to end on anyway, and going, 'All right, mate, 500.'

You're engaging in this ancient ritual. Sometimes (okay, often) I will sell something for less than I bought it for. Why? Because I just enjoy the transaction that much, and I have connected with the guy who wants it. And I think, 'All right, he's here, he got out of bed, he might as well have it, and I'll make up that fifteen quid on something else.' So, I take the cash over, he's happy and I'm happy. I'd rather do that than go away thinking I've ripped someone off. If you rip someone off, right, then the curse is on you, not on the geezer who finds that the engine's made of marmalade when he gets it home. The curse of being a bad'un, it's on you, man. It's not a joke when you rip someone off because it's in your soul. You've got to take that to the grave; you cleaned that poor sod out.

And when you return to your shed, those bad feelings will follow you, and they have no place in a shed, unless you're making methamphetamine in your shed in which case, as previously noted, get a lock-up for your nasty, nefarious business because we don't want anything to do with you. I don't want any part of it. I believe that a shed should be a spiritual, honest place where you can come and be proud of yourself.

14:
Why Shopping in Sheds Is Good for Your Soul

I was listening to a mate of mine talk about this American wealth guru podcaster the other day, and he was saying that the guru says money is more complicated, and perhaps more spiritual, than we think it is. He was basically saying that money is this almost-mystical energy force – like heat, or light, or power or time. I mean, it was clearly mumbo-jumbo and he said the podcast ended up by trying to get you to buy some course off him, but what I do believe is that hanging out at auto jumbles does make you understand that money is not just a means of exchange; it's also a means of communication with your fellow man.

Apparently one of the best things people with depression can do is go to a jumble sale for a rummage. The whole concept of having to talk to somebody, haggle with somebody, get your money out, be engaged with somebody and look somebody in the eye is just so valuable for us as humans. These days, we kind of think that buying and selling is just about buying and selling, but it's actually not. It's also about all that stuff around buying and selling. It's actually about interacting with your fellow humans.

Wheeling and dealing is incredibly therapeutic. It engages you with other people, but also it generates self-worth because if you spot a knackered old petrol can, right, and you buy it for a fiver, and then you take it home, and you clean it with Pledge, and you spray some WD-40 on the brass top and get it off, get it working, polish it up, and then you take it back to another auto jumble and you sell it for twenty quid – well, that's a tidy profit but far from making you rich, so it's definitely not all about the money.

Yes, it's about adding value to that can, but it's actually about adding value to my sense of self-worth and my soul; I've taken something, and through my interaction with it, I've actually created something that is better than when I first had it and the money is the proof of that. It's a way of keeping track of how effectively you are making things better. And when you sell a can for twenty quid that you bought for a fiver and fixed up to make it actually worth twenty quid, you feel as though you've achieved something. You feel like you just put the ball in the back of the net, son. And you look at the can sitting on the bench and you think, 'I've done something good here. I've waxed that can, and it looks lovely. I've saved it from oblivion.'

But actually making money wheeling and dealing is tough. One way to do it to observe the old adage, 'Buy up north, sell down south.' Buy from the people who know where it's at up north and sell to the people who are slightly richer down south. That works, there's about a 20 per cent margin.

You buy a tractor up north for 1,500 quid, you can sell it for 2,200 down south. And then if you really want to get a bargain, go on a shed rummage in Ireland. I mean, the Emerald Isle is the best place in the world to find stuff in sheds. The people are great, the tea is great and the deals are great. I get seriously excited when we have a trip to Ireland on the wallchart.

And if it's different in Ireland, then head further west to America and it's a totally different ball game. The critical difference between UK sheds and US sheds is size. American sheds are normally much, much bigger than UK sheds, but because we've been knocking around for longer, the sheds that we have here in the UK often contain items that date from before America even really got going. In America, because their history is just that bit younger than ours, you ain't going to be finding a Georgian chest of drawers or a grandfather clock from the 1700s. The stuff that you find in American sheds is much more about pop culture than antiquity, on the whole, but that suits me down to the ground. The Americans have the most unbelievable kit in their sheds, and I yearn to go and have a proper rummage in all that Americana.

The shed in America has culturally been part of the psyche for a long time, partly just because they had the space and the money. Fifteen, twenty years ago, you weren't seen as a weirdo if you collected loads of stuff in America, but you definitely were here, and still are to an extent. Shed dwelling has been, and remains, quite sub-cultural in the UK; people are still kind of shy about telling you they have a shed full of petrol pumps, or whatever. But in the US I feel it's more acceptable.

And while you very rarely see collections of, let's say, cinema memorabilia in sheds in the UK, you do the whole time in the US. They dig much deeper into pop culture in what they stash. For instance, there are loads of sheds out there full of pinball machines, or you'll find the most incredible Star Wars collection or a Ninja Turtle collection or a Star Trek collection, but on a much, much bigger level to anything you would find here. They've embraced the heritage of their recent pop culture, whereas we have done that less so. So, scale is really what it's all about in America, and as a result, the sheds people have are vast.

One of the great things about rummaging in America is that prices are much more reasonable than here in the UK. Another is that some of the automotive stuff that we hanker for here was so ubiquitous over there that not only do you find it in sheds, but they normally have an awful lot of detritus composting in their gardens in America. You'll go to some guy's house and he'll have not one quintessential American pick-up, but rows of them. Over here they're cherished; over there they're discarded. So, even though they know that they're historical and they know that they are classics, in America they're basically thirteen to the dozen.

People will tell you that we've ravaged all their bone-yards; we haven't even touched the sides, man. The reality is that millions of the great Japanese motorcycles and British motorcycles were exported to America, and it was very much a throwaway society, so consequently you did 5,000 miles on your Kawasaki Z9, and then it would just be left at a mate's house if it broke down. They'd just go and get another one, whereas we'd be trying to fix it with balsa wood and some UHU glue, because we were broke and it was our only means of transport. In fact, it is estimated that 75 per cent of all those classic British motorcycles of the pre-1990s were exported to America. There are millions of them out there waiting to be brought back to life again.

And that's the critical thing to understand about a junking trip to America (or, more accurately these days, American websites). When it comes to pop-cultural finds, you can eat your heart out but they know what they have got. But for the more recent automotive history, for American, British and Japanese stuff, then America's where it's at because the stuff is just not valued. If you want to find yourself some very cheap Triumph engines, buy them in from America, not from the UK. When it comes to Italian cars and all that kind of stuff, then Europe is the place to be still. Fiats and Ferraris and all that kind of stuff; if that's your poison, then Europe is still your hunting ground. But if it's American, British or Japanese stuff you want, then I really would suggest looking west, especially when it comes to motorcycles.

I would love to go on a mission for the ultimate barn finds, with Sammy, which encompasses the world, not only America. The simple fact is that 3,000 Brough Superiors were made, but only 1,500 are accounted for. Now, supposedly there are Broughs in Argentina, there're Broughs in South East Asia. Wouldn't it be great to go on a mission to find some of those lost ones in those sheds? (Sounds like a TV show, where's my agent?!) I think that's every shed dweller's dream. It would be amazing to find something like that.

One thing that normal people don't really get is that there are sheds all over the world, filled with fascinating stuff, some of it valuable, some of it not. People have been stashing stuff internationally, whether it's in India or Indianapolis, and it is all just waiting to be discovered. From time to time, ten to fifteen million quid cars come out of barn finds, often in deepest Bavaria or somewhere like that. I mean there's probably even a shed in Greenland filled with rare Skidoos. You just never know and that's the excitement of the thing.

When I get any item that I have acquired back to my shed, my booty, whether it be from Ireland or America or Cornwall, I'll add monetary value but the value that I'll add is completely secondary in importance to the value that I'll derive spiritually, just from doing what goes on in a shed.

As a semi-pro shed dweller, making dollar means you get to own the item for a bit and enjoy it in your shed, but it also means you can justify keeping going to yourself and the wife, even though she knows of course, just like you do, that on a pure profit and loss basis, the justification for describing this as a moneymaking venture is wafer thin to say the least. The money is a means of validating the work that I've done, although of course there are a small band of professional jumblers, and they do indeed make money, quite a lot of it sometimes if they know what they are about.

But that guy you see every week, who has made it a career, he didn't start off as a professional. He started off as a guy getting a can and getting a kick out of quadrupling its value. Auto jumbles are a microcosm of life, and you can tell, I think, a lot about the jumblers from their wares. A jumbler's stall tells an awful lot about the person. Over the years, what you love changes, and so consequently a jumble is not just an extension of someone's psyche but also a kind of biographical exercise as well.

For success at a jumble, if you're going to be even semi-professional, you need to specialize in something, so people turn up and they go, 'Oh Henry, he does WLA Harley parts.' So, you go to Henry's stall, and you know that Henry will have original front wheels, original mags, original whatever for a WLA or Harleys of that era, and you can't get that on the high street.

If you are just starting out in jumbling, you are probably selling a huge variety of quite random stuff, which is good because you are broadening your horizons in terms of potential punters, but ultimately you have to specialize. Because if you're coming to a specialist stall at Kempton, right, for Northern parts, you're expecting to pay good money for those parts because you're going to the specialist who's got the rare stuff.

But of course, a general motorbike jumble stall, that has everything to do with motorbikes and petrol cans and whatever, that's where the bargains happen, the jumblers who've cleared out five or six sheds, right, and they've put it all on a trestle table, literally poured it out, like Sam does, they pour it out and sit and wait and when you pick up anything you get the same reply: 'That's a fiver, son, but call it two quid.' Whatever. Because it's just an array of detritus, right? He has just got to get rid of it. The people who have a general offering are the meat and potatoes of the jumble, but if you're specializing in tin signs, enamel signs, right, then you're going to walk up to that stall knowing that the geezer knows exactly what it is firstly, exactly how much it is worth and also the guy's going to be a hard-nosed sausage to negotiate with.

But then I've seen the general jumble people, after a while go, 'Actually, hang on, those wheel rims sell, those beaded edged rims. So what happens if I specialize in them?' For me and Sammy, even in the short period we've done *Junk & Disorderly*, we are finding that people are coming to us for tin cans, signs and memorabilia, and then obviously the odd motorbike. So we now have two departments at a jumble. I deal with the memorabilia, and all that kind of stuff and the cans, because I know a lot about it, and Sammy sells the motorbikes and the big stuff.

The auto jumble is one of the last places where unreconstructed males can hang out and not feel guilty or inadequate about being who they are. A jumble is also the place where you meet other shed dwellers and discover the things they care about. We are kindred spirits. It doesn't matter whether the guy is selling 1950s bar stools or he's selling Brough Superior parts; we're all in it together. We're all there to immerse ourselves in this extension of shed dwelling.

That said, the smashed avocado boys and girls, they do turn up to jumbles sometimes. They're like beacons. You can see them coming, and you think, aye-aye, here we go, eh? Have a can to put your diced walnuts in, you know? You clock them as they're coming down the aisle, looking for something to furnish their café in east London, and good luck to them. They are welcome, their cash is welcome, their interest in automotive history is welcome and if they've made the effort to come out to a jumble, they are 99 per cent top people.

That is the thing about sheds and jumbling; it's classless. It doesn't matter whether you're a duke or a dustman, you have a right to be there, firstly. And secondly, you have no right to be arrogant. You have no right to believe that you are above the person selling the detritus, or the person who's selling V-twin engines at twenty-five grand a pop. The point is, we are all a community of equals. And this is what I love about life in a shed and a day at a jumble; it doesn't matter where I'm from, I can just be me. The keeping up with the Joneses, the giving it huge, the showing off; there's no place for it.

I mean, there are people I see at jumbles who are alcoholics, right, and they're sitting there with a bottle of Newcastle Brown, and you look at their stall and it's just a disaster. It has bits of stuff everywhere, there's broken handlebars, bent levers, whatever. It's just a pile of junk, right? And the geezer's sitting there on a stool, with a bottle of Newky Brown and a dog that hasn't been fed for three weeks, and a van that is basically composting in front of his eyes. And you think to yourself, 'This guy's really got to get off the booze, then he might have something decent to sell.' But he doesn't. And isn't that fantastic? Next month: 'There's that geezer again with the detritus. He hasn't sold those spare wheels in four years, but he's still here.' Yes, and the beauty of a jumble is that he has every right to be, just as much as me or Sam or the guy with the perfectly ordered collection of Healey light bulbs.

I always sell knowing that the person who I'm selling it to is going to mark it up again. And I always say, 'You know, mate, I understand, we've got to leave a little bit of a roof on it for you.' Take my old Chopper GT Sprint that I had kicking about in the shed for about a year. It's a Chopper bicycle with drop handlebars, and they are almost unheard of. They made very few of them, because no one wanted to buy them. Why would you make a Chopper – *a Chopper*, right – with drop handlebars? But they tried it, and made a few, and as a result they are as rare as hen's teeth. I bought it off a geezer for £1,175, which was a good price, but top spec retail it's probably worth £2,000. But then I had a guy ring me the other day and say, 'Henry, I'll give you 1,500 for that Chopper GT,' I thought, well, okay, maybe. I didn't try and sell it to this geezer. He just rang up because a mate of a mate of ours knew that I had it. If I sell it to him for £1,500, right, I'm making £325, so, happy days. I'm just making a quick flip. SPQR: Small Profit Quick Return, as Arthur Daley said. The Chopper is worth two grand and I know he'll advertise it for two grand and probably get it. But he's got to advertise it. He's got to entertain all the tyre kickers. He's got to have all the people coming round drinking tea on a Saturday and he deserves 500 quid more for doing that. And he deserves 500 quid because we're both working together in the service of a larger goal, which is keeping the whole damn show on the road.

And I think you need to approach life that way as well. It's not about who you can screw. It's not about rinsing everybody for the last penny. There will always be someone who's going to be richer and thinner than you, or making a few quid more than you, and once you understand that, and you understand it doesn't matter, you can enjoy the simple fact of being alive. And that comes from being in a shed, because in a shed you're taking away all that aspirational materialism and replacing it with the environment you want to create, you want to be in and you feel safe in. You're creating a world of your own where nobody will come in, unless you invite them in (unless they've got a crowbar and a hoody and then that's a different story).

I think the sense of a larger good is the key difference between a car boot sale and an auto jumble. You see, a car boot sale really is about money. Let's be honest, you're trying to skank people for your broken electronics and your foot spa that you never opened four Christmases ago. It's a job of work to actually get rid of, for really any price at all, junk that you have amassed and don't want, detritus that holds no resonance emotionally to you because it's been in the loft along with your Cabbage Patch Dolls in their original box which are worth a tenner.

It's a more cynical exercise, it hasn't got the camaraderie. And I think there's no camaraderie (that I can make out, anyway) because it's not derived from a hobby. The car boot sale is the physical manifestation of the emotional sickness of just insatiably wanting. You have acquired all these things you wanted but didn't need, through social pressure, or a desire to impress, or advertising, and now you want to get rid of them and get the money back. So you've got a deep fat fryer, a big lean frying machine, a set of hair irons you've been given, a camping sink you gave to someone else and they've given it back to you, it's just basically gone through their hands and changed the wrapping. So, while a car boot sale has got the excitement of turning inanimate objects into cash, what it doesn't have, I think, is the passion and love.

An auto jumble is also a bit of a competition and a bit of a game, a bit of fun where you can leverage your knowledge to get a deal. I have done some great deals in my time, and some crap ones. I bought a Brough Superior for fifty grand, and I sold it for ninety. But, as I said earlier, I also bought two new Lamborghini Countachs for eighty-five and ninety-five grand respectively, sold them for seventy-five and eighty-five, and now they'd be worth half a million quid each.

So, like a lot of shed dwellers, I'd rather talk about my gains than my losses. I go to sheds and buy stuff, and normally I'll make money out of most things I buy, and I'm buying stuff at the lower end: maybe the odd four grand Harley or five grand Triumph, but mostly it's tin signs for fifty quid.

Signs are a great thing to get into. I remember one of the best signs I bought, for 125 quid, was a Cyclist's Touring Club sign from the turn of the century. They are very rare and they have a great history. Back in the day, in Edwardian times, hotels didn't allow cyclists in because cyclists were generally plebs and commoners, and maybe thieves. So, these signs, the Cyclist Touring Club signs, were put outside bed and breakfasts because they accepted cyclists. And mine is a really rare sign which I have restored and cleaned and looked after, and it's now probably worth a grand.

So that's my kind of sweet spot I guess, buying stuff for a couple of hundred – 300, 400, 700 – selling it for a grand, whatever it may be. The big stuff hasn't generally come out of sheds if I'm honest. It's mainly off the Internet. Like there's a guy in Phoenix with a Mustang GT500, and the guy wants $90,000 for it, and I reckon it's worth 160K sterling, and I'm trying to buy it at the moment. So online there can be good business decisions, but the transactions are stripped of humanity.

It's the shed stuff that I actually get excited about. It's that moment where you find some old bike with the engine falling out of it and you sort it out and resell it and you just feel you're doing your bit that actually brings me real joy. Like, I found a lovely old Royal Enfield sign the other day: it's double-sided and it bolts to the wall. It was knackered when I bought it, so I got it for 125 quid, but I have spent ages fixing it and restoring it and honestly, now, I wouldn't take less than £1,500 for it. So, it's those kinds of deals that I absolutely love.

I've never once intentionally ripped anyone off. If I have bought a garage sign for 200 quid and done nothing to it, I would sell it for 300. I'm making a hundred. Of course, I'm making a hundred. But Doug who I bought it off, he knows that and that's why he sold it to me for 200 rather than going, 'Sorry, mate, it's 300 and that's it.' And the guy

I flogged it to can make another hundred as well. It's about cash flow. It's about enjoying it for a bit and then moving the stock around. Simples.

The bottom line is that you've got to be fair. Otherwise the shed isn't a good place to be. Because if stuff has come out of your shed and you're ripping people off when people have come into your shed, it's bad man. It's not a good shed. It's bad sheddery.

The Holy Grail of shed rummaging used to be that you'd go into a shed, and there, amid all the reams of trinketry and loveliness and defunct threshing machinery, you'd see a distinctive set of handlebars poking up from under a ripped old tarpaulin and just from the shape of them you'd know it was a Brough Superior. So, then, in your fantasy, you'd spend another few minutes wandering around the place, trying to act cool and keeping your powder dry. Emotionally, the goal when faced with a potential classic shed acquisition like that is to be flatlining.

So, eventually, you wander back over to the ripped tarp and sort of pull it back, stick your nose in. He goes, 'That's a nice bike, that is.' 'Oh, really, what is it?' you say. 'I'm not sure, my uncle dumped it here, I think he said it was called a something-inferior.' 'Oh yeah, is it? I've never heard of them. Anyway, what's that over there? An old milk churn? And you know, those tin signs are lovely, how much do you want for them mate?' Then you'd talk about the tin signs and the milk churns for a bit and then at the last minute you'd glance back over to the bike and say, 'Well, I guess I could take the bike as well.'

At least, that was the approach twenty years ago for everything in sheds. You'd go in, you'd kind of pretend that you didn't really know what you were looking at and give the impression of, 'It's all lovely but, you know, it doesn't affect me, but, okay, twist my arm.' Well, the Internet has put paid to a lot of that. Because, now, obviously, he's googled everything in the place and he's pricing what he's got against the perfectly restored one on eBay. So now, if you go, 'Do you want to sell those signs?' I guarantee the first thing he will say is: 'Well, I don't know, if you could afford them, Henry, I've seen one on eBay for 400 quid.' And then you are totally scuppered.

It doesn't matter that the guy who stuck it on eBay is never going to get £400 for his sign, and it doesn't matter that the one on eBay is in perfect condition, immaculately restored and hanging on the wall of an antiques shop in Primrose Hill, and this guy has a stack of rusty signs with a few bottles of weedkiller perched on top, leaking poisonous effluent onto them, because he now has that number in his head. Your problem, especially if he doesn't actually really need the money, is that anything less than £400 is now going to feel like a disappointment.

For some reason, people believe that just because they've seen a fully restored Triumph Bonneville for twelve and a half grand, that their total rust bucket is worth ten. What is that? It's worth two and a half, because I'm going to have to spend ten doing it up, and even then I'll be lucky to get twelve and a half for it.

So although I still feel a lot of excitement about going

into a new shed, because that fundamental hit of, 'Oh, my God, look at all this stuff,' is still there, that lasts a very short time when you suddenly realize by the glint in the bloke's eye that he knows what every single bloody item is, and what it could be worth in his dreams. That, for the shed dweller, is a majorly depressive situation, because you are not going to have the fun of owning that little bit of whatever it may be for a couple of months until you flog it on to the next geezer, because you just won't be able to make a profit on it. The only way nowadays to get a nice little deal out of a shed, to break the eBay spell, is to buy in bulk and buy in cash. You absolutely have to be holding the folding, and as much of it as possible.

In this scenario, you go into the shed, and there are like twenty tin signs, and you say to the geezer, 'How much do you want for all of them?' And he's a bit surprised and he goes, 'Oh, I don't know.' And then you come back with a good, fair, ready-money offer: 'I'll give you £2,000, cash, and I've got it here in my pocket.' 'Have you?' he says. Maybe you get it out and smack your hand with it, let the weight of that cash really do some talking. 'Blimey. Oh . . . oh . . . oh, maybe then, yeah, okay, let's do it Henry.' That is the way to beat eBay. A fistful of wedge.

So, while the colour of the money will always soften someone up, and the days are over of walking out with a tin sign for a tenner, or a petrol pump for a hundred quid, there are deals to be had out there, and fundamentally the enjoyment of searching in a shed is still about being able to leverage your own little bit of specialist knowledge. Yes, specialist knowledge isn't perhaps quite as valuable as it used to be, because anyone can just google anything, but when you get into really specialist shed stuff, Google hits a brick wall, because it's mainly interested in the preoccupations of avocado-eaters, such as where to get the best flat white, which is usually quite a long way away from your average shed.

But I think it's important to say that when you go into a shed on a shed search, and you go in there having got quite a lot of knowledge and hoping that you have more knowledge than the person's shed that you're in, it's not about ripping people off. You don't go into an old boy's shed thinking, 'I'm going to have him.' If you do find a Triumph Bonneville 1959, and offer the geezer two grand and he takes it, well, I speak for myself, I just couldn't be doing that. Ripping people off is un-brotherly, and, actually a shed search becomes an even more joyful occasion when the other guy has knowledge too, because then actually you might learn something and get to feel good about yourself. So, at the end of the day, I actually like that situation when people are really engaged and educated in the contents of their shed because actually you can probably get a fair price from them in that scenario rather than a ridiculously inflated price.

It's usually quite obvious, when you ask a few questions, which I always do, just how much knowledge that person whose shed you are in has. The minute he's going, 'Well, it's an overhead Cam from 1934, and I really do love these Cammy Nortons because the model 18 came out in . . .' then while you're not going to get something for nothing you might get something even more valuable, which is more knowledge. But, assuming it feels like the distribution of knowledge is more or less even, then you can start to think, 'We're in with a shout here.'

Then, the way to get a good deal, is to be really, really well-versed on the detail. So, if you go into a shed with Sammy, yeah, Sam will go, 'Oh, those lugs on that bike, Jesus, those are works lugs on the frame, they're fretted lugs, and blimey, that's a bronze head on that engine, so this could be a works racer.'

I think the other thing that is really going to stand you in good stead in a shed is to be able to make an educated guess about just how hard something is going to be to get going. A lot of mechanical stuff in sheds ain't ticking over, mainly because the bloke who owns it has not got the time or the interest to get it ticking over, so, that's another great way to get deals, because chances are he wouldn't mind it gone anyway because it's just sitting there reminding him of his own frailty as a human being. If you have a little bit of confidence in your own ability, then you are able to say, 'Well, you know, chances are I can unseize the engine,' or, 'Maybe it's just a fuse,' and that gives you the confidence to pick up stuff that other people wouldn't touch. For instance, Sam and I picked up a lovely little Velocette in a shed for *Junk & Disorderly*. It was completely knackered and the engine literally fell out of it as we wheeled it into the van. But we changed the magneto and got it running, and sold it on as a project.

Knowledge is power in sheds. Back in the day, you didn't really have to have that much knowledge. If you knew it was a Triumph Bonneville T120, 1970, then you knew that was the one to have and you were off to the races. Now, you have to know a bit more even for basic shed finds.

So, that's the bad side of the Internet, but I do understand it from the seller's point of view: you think you have a rare bike, and you're not sure, so you stick it on eBay and then other people may realize what Sammy would have realized and you get a global bidding war, which you would never have before. A huge amount of that kind of rare stuff is bought by people abroad, and you'd never reach some of the markets that you can doing it online, and that in itself is good, but I have personally just had so many nightmares with online sales that I don't put anything on eBay anymore because you just get so many tyre kickers.

Like, I had a Ford Anglia about ten years ago that I got out of a shed. I put it on eBay for two and a half grand. The description was absolutely spot-on; really, really detailed of how messed up it was, stains here, corroded there, paint chips everywhere. A guy bought it and came to pick it up. And the guy turned up and he goes, 'That don't look what I thought it would look like?' I go: 'What do you mean by that? We told you exactly what it was. Exactly.' Anyway, to cut a long story short, the guy starts trying to haggle with me after having bought it and in the end he gets in his car and heads off and I sold it to a proper shed dweller, face to face, old style.

Non-shed dwellers don't really get it. I had another one

the other day. This geezer turns up and he wants a VFR750 Honda which I want to sell. He turns up on a Saturday morning, about ten o'clock and he first of all starts by lining up the front wheel and the rear wheel, you know, like a snooker player about to take a shot, looking at the wheels. I go, 'What are you doing?' He goes, 'Oh, I'm just checking for wheel alignment.' I go, 'What? It's 750 quid, mate. They are pointing the same way, that's as good as it gets.' Then he wanders about for a bit and then he goes, 'Oh, there's a crack on that . . .' 'Yeah,' I said, 'that's because it's been thrown down the road both sides, like I told you.'

'Well, I better take it for a test ride then.' I go, 'Are you insured?' He goes, 'Well I don't know.' And I said, 'Well, you better put my trade plates on then.' So I give him a trade plate, and off he goes. For forty minutes. Just when I'm thinking he's crashed into a hedge and I'm going to have to send a search party out, he comes back, and he goes, 'It rides nice.' I said, 'It's going to ride nice. I told you it was. I'm not lying to you. I've told you exactly what's wrong with it.' He goes: 'Oh, well, you know, I . . . well I'll think about it.' So, off he goes! Well, to give him his due, he did have the courtesy to email me back, and he said, 'No, I'm not going to buy it, because it won't fit in my garden.'

That's when I realized my fundamental mistake: He wasn't even a shed dweller! He hasn't got a shed and he hasn't actually got a clue because if you don't have a shed and you want to buy a classic vehicle, you're definitely not firing on both brain cells because it's just going to compost in your garden or get nicked. Build a shed first, then go out and find your dream vehicle. Sheds are the precursor to heaven. Don't try and get your heaven without putting in the hard work of building a shed first. Otherwise you're a goon.

Now, the one thing I will say about the online market-places is that they can be quite handy if you've got to find some random part. That is where eBay is utterly, utterly incredible and I probably buy something five days out of seven off eBay, but it's nearly all small stuff. Like, for instance, I had a Corvette Stingray, and it was in concourse condition apart from there was one rubber bung missing on the toast rack; that's the luggage rack at the back of the boot. Without eBay where would you find that? Impossible, nearly. But type in: 'rubber bung, luggage rack, Corvette 1972' and up it comes, a bag of them for four quid. Add to basket, and it's done, innit? Comes from America a week later. Joy! My vehicle is now properly concourse. I mean, you would have spent days on the phone trying to find that, so, buying parts online for your restoration is an utter godsend.

Now, the one very obvious problem is that you can't actually physically check the parts and a lot of them are repro, modern-made stuff, and you just don't know till it comes over if it's going to work because no one's ever tried to fit it. They may have just made it from a template from something that probably wasn't quite right in the first place, so there's always that worry and that's why there is nothing sweeter than finding the missing part at an auto jumble where you can pick it up and peer at it.

The Internet definitely has curtailed the numbers of people coming to auto jumbles. For me an auto jumble is an event, and it's an event that I cherish every week. But for other people, they're coming to actually look for a specific part and in that case the sad truth is you're probably better off looking online. But it's a bit like when they started televising the Premier League, that would have killed the matches, so they keep a few matches back. Auto jumbles are the same, there's some magic kept back just for the auto jumble by the shed gods, I think.

The real problem with the Internet is that it doesn't allow for the whole concept of drinking tea. Whenever you turn up to a shed, the guy doesn't ever want to sell anything. But he's got some lovely pieces, and he's a good lad, so you don't give up. You say, 'Shall we go and see Derek again, Sammy? What do you reckon? He's just up the way from where we are. Shall we go and have another cup of tea with him?' So, you go back two or three times to drink tea, yeah, not to bore the geezer, but just to pop in and say 'Hi', have a cup of tea, shoot the breeze, whatever, because he is a decent bloke with an amazing shed. And then after you've drunk tea about three times, you may go to the back of his shed and go, 'Derek, look mate, won't you sell this BSA to me?' 'Oh, I don't know, Henry, what would you offer me?' And I would go, 'What do you reckon it's worth?' And he goes, 'I reckon that's six grand.' I go, 'Well look, I've got cash, what about four?' He goes, 'Oh, go on, as long as you make the next tea.'

And you've got a deal! And what's more, it's a fair deal. He knows that I'm going to sell it on and probably need to make 1,500 quid on it, and there's going to be a bit of cleaning up and the odd spare part. So, he's selling at a fair price to me and I'm selling at a fair price to the next guy and we're all getting to roam around the country in our vans, drinking tea with each other and you can't drink tea online. It's when you drink tea and you're talking to a like-minded fella that you get a result. It's like people come over here, I make them tea, we go to the shed, we chat. And I have no intention of selling them anything, and then they go, 'How much is that Chopper Mark 1 bicycle, Henry? Do you want to flog that?' 'Not really, mate.' 'Come on, I'll give you 600 quid for it.' 'Oh, all right.'

So, yes, the Internet is great but I do think for the serious shed dweller it will never give you the spiritual satisfaction of face-to-face deal-making. It doesn't do that in any way.

15:
The World Is Changing Fast. Should I Open the Shed Door?

My shed is a totally guilt-free environment, and, consequently, when I'm here tinkering away with my petrol cans or my seventies Chopper, I sometimes get nervous about the outside world.

To be really honest, I struggle with the future and seek solace in the past. I am fearful of the future because the world is changing so fast. I think it's all going too quick, and I don't always know who or what to be in it.

So the best solution is to hang out with my mates, and stay in the world of sheds, auto jumbles and auctions. That is my world and I'm very happy to let someone else have a go at shaping the new one.

I genuinely find myself, when the wife's gone to bed, sneaking downstairs and watching those music channels filled with seventies and eighties music promos. I love the eclectic mix of music, clothes, styles and the old rockers giving it rock all. It's safe, it ain't gonna change, and it's what the world was like when I was ready to take on that world. Forty years later I've made my bed (but not in a shed, as per the Commandments).

It's been a rocky road at times, but I've loved it and am proud in my small way of what I've created with the help of my wife and mates but I think twice now about opening the shed door. I might not be able to close it again, you know?

The Covid-19 lockdown made me think long and hard about what life is all about. It made me think about what really matters to me, and I mean really matters.

I have been appreciating the little things, but *really* appreciating them.

A great cuppa tea, a beautiful rose climbing the shed, the pie crust tank on my Norton, the panel fit on my Corvette. All the things that I miss and ignore when the stress of the outside world comes knocking on the shed door.

But lockdown has been a roller coaster of emotions as well; friends have been sick, friends have died.

I regularly found myself with tears in my eyes and I'd just think, what the hell has happened? Lockdown has proved to me that I should fear the future, and it's taking time to figure out how to deal with it.

I'm dealing with it by chatting to friends, my long-suffering wife Janie and my boys Charlie and Tom. I do also seek solace in the company of my dog Jellybean, because she too is very much part of my rehabilitation post lockdown.

But above all what I have needed is a safe place to just be in, and for me, guess what, the shed is where it's at. No one's playing Fortnite in a shed or hassling Janie about what's for lunch or whether they can see friends – 'No, its bloody lockdown!' – peace and serenity have a chance in a shed, even in lockdown times.

My love of the past has got me wondering whether you could run a farm in the old way but still make it financially viable. I'd love to do that as an experiment; get in my shed and restore or fettle a load of classic farm machinery, combines, tractors, my 135 Massey, my 65 Massey, my trail-ploughs, my old Bamford balers, all that kind of stuff and see whether I could make money running a smallholding with classic vehicles. Like all shed dwellers, I feel the place to really see our classic vehicles is back in action – whether that's on the road or on a farm, fully restored, working, actually doing a job.

Another good thing about having a shed in these strange times is that the last thing most shed dwellers want to do for a holiday is to get on a plane.

I want to go to the shed for my holidays, not least because I don't want to be sitting on some foreign beach with a virus raging, thinking, 'How do I get out of here?'

I understand that people sometimes have to travel for business, to make a few quid, and I can understand it if you're going to go to France to ride some great roads or going to Morocco to go surfing or kite flying or have some specific experience *that can only be had in that place.* But what I don't understand is travel for the sake of it, to sit on one of those boring beaches. 'Where did you go?' 'Oh, we went to Lanzarote.' 'Oh, we went to Croatia, it's much nicer.' 'Where did you go Henry?' 'I went to my shed.'

Incidentally, what is it about beaches and the global

mindfulness industry? Why are the gurus so obsessed about being on a beach to be spiritually contented? What's so good about the noise of the waves? Beaches: there's nothing to eat. There's no shade. If you lay out there long enough, you're going to be dead. You've got sand up your crack, your whole body is just waiting for some kid to run past and make a shadow across your face and fling sand on you and a seagull could bombard you with guano at any moment. 'You are on a deserted beach . . .' What's that about? You can't get an ice cream; you can't go into a beachside café. All it is, is sand. For thousands of miles. And blue water. Which in a way obviously is nice, but after about three minutes, it's even nicer to get back on the bike.

You don't need to be a guru to understand that the most rewarding journey is the one you make into your own soul, and for some people that journey might happen with a book under a tree in the garden, or tending their cabbage patch, but for shed dwellers it happens at the workbench. In your shed, you're self-motivating, you're self-creating and you're getting to know yourself a little better, and becoming a better person; so get yourself a shed and forget the airmiles.

I found out a long time ago that wherever you go, you take yourself with you, and the beauty of the shed is that instead of encouraging you to run away from yourself, like all the package holiday adverts and game shows, it allows you to find freedom by fully being and expressing yourself as a man. So then, two hours later, you can come out of the shed and go back into the kitchen a better person.

I think sheds make you a better person because there is something utterly spiritually fulfilling about completing even the simplest repair job, like changing the fuse on a toaster. I mean, I think we'd be amazed if we accurately knew how many electrical appliances are chucked out each day for want of a fuse. When you scale that up to the concept of restoration, or just simply getting something going, well, it's a hugely fulfilling thing because you are testing yourself. You are being patient, you're being tolerant and you're stepping out of your comfort zone a lot of the time as you attempt new challenges as you grow in confidence.

So when you strip that carburettor, that looked at first sight incredibly complex, which you've never done before, the fulfilment you get from having achieved it is phenomenal, especially if the bike runs sweetly after doing it. That is a hugely fulfilling thing to do. It's a revelation to most people the first time, that you can really do your soul some serious good by fixing material objects that you just don't get if you chucked the thing out and bought a lovely shiny new one.

Fixing is the absolute opposite of materialism, it's the fetishization of frugality rather than consumption. That sense of make do and mend, of not wasting, is at the absolute core of shed dwelling. When I take an old bike down to the shed, stick it on the workbench, put the tea on and actually try and fix it, I feel like I'm giving two fingers to all the stuff I hate in this world: conspicuous consumption, boasting, *Love Island*, waste, adverts, people trying to tell me how to live my life.

At the beginning, probably five times out of ten, you don't manage to fix it and you lob it. Non-shed dwellers would say you wasted a day and should just go and buy a new one, but they're so wrong because actually you've done something incredible; you've given it a go. You've done your best and, in sheds, as in life, you do your best and then try and let go of the result.

Of course, it makes you horribly unsatisfied when you fail. You've stripped that carburettor, you put it back on the bike and there's two bolts on the workbench and you've no idea where they've come from. How many times has that happened to me! That is a really bad day. It really is. I'm not minimizing the frustration and anger and irritation that can cause, but it's just absolutely vital how you react to that failure. Do you start throwing stuff around? Do you burn the shed to the ground? Or do you take a deep breath, go back up the garden path to the house, read *Classic Tractor* magazine and come back revitalized the next day and have another go?

Fixing stuff, or trying to, is for me a parable of the way you are choosing to live your life and sometimes it takes a bit of effort to be a better person.

For my parents' generation, fixing stuff was totally normal. That was not just because they had less stuff. The bottom line is that they were taught not to waste stuff, it's the same principle as pushing food round your plate when you were a kid: 'Eat your veg, you're not having any ice cream if you don't eat your swede.' Now it's like, 'Forget the swede, and as for that clogged vacuum cleaner, let's lob it rather than unblocking it.'

Back in the seventies, even the eighties, it was engrained in us to look after things and fix things. Owning something came with an understanding that you were going to be maintaining something. And because you weren't going to get a new car after three years of repayments, you were going to keep that car you bought for all of your life and possibly your kids would have it after your death, you got to know it, you got to understand it, you had a relationship with it. You knew when she was ill, you even knew when she was *about* to be ill, and you did something about it. It was an amazingly fulfilling experience, actually, maintaining and living with an item, whether it was a toaster or a fridge or a Rolls-Royce.

The throwaway society does the opposite. It doesn't indoctrinate people to cherish the objects they have, to look after that stuff and live their lives with it and understand that it's an extension of you, and how you treat it and care for it reflects on you as a human. It says to them, 'Just get a new one.'

Do you know Ikea are now selling lights in which you cannot change the bulb? When the bulb runs out, throw the whole item away. How did we get to that place that it was cheaper not to change a bulb than to change a bulb? I mean, how did that happen?

I am uneasy about a future where you can't fix stuff, you just throw it away instead, and it's happening to everything now, not just cars. When your washing machine broke down, even a few years ago, you'd be able to call a local fixer man, and this guy would come round and fix it. He'd be there with his head in the back of the cupboard and his arse hanging out of his trousers, pulling the thing out and going, 'Oh, yeah, it's just this bit of rubber here that turns the drum, it's knackered, I've got one in the van.'

Well, the other day the tumble drier packed up. Can we find someone to come and look at it? No. There's no one here. One guy who we used has moved to Cornwall, probably because in my experience that's an area where there are still some people who value keeping older machines going rather than thinking, 'Well, he's going to charge 75 quid to come out and look at it. Then he's going to order the part. Then he's going to come back a couple of days later and fit the part, call that a week. So, all that hassle and probably it's going to in total cost 150 quid. Let's just buy another for 200.'

16:
Men and the
Art of Motorcycle
Maintenance

I suppose the overarching thing I've learnt in sheds on the technical skills side, is simply how to get a vehicle that looks like it is totally finished going again. I also have developed the ability, which is really important when you're rummaging in sheds, to troubleshoot accurately.

If a bike won't start, I know quite a few things to try now that might make it do just that. Like, you know, checking for a spark. If not, is there a coil? Is the magneto broken? You go through all the processes and eliminate things; if you've got a spark, and it's not running, it must be a fuel issue, so, let's check the pilot jet and the main jet of the carburettor. Are they blocked? Do we need to strip the carb? (The answer to this question always seems to be yes.) And if the carb seems okay, then maybe the issue is further back. Is fuel actually getting to the carburettor?

I'd be fairly confident now that I can sort out the top end of a bike. I can't weld very well yet, but I'm learning; that's the next thing I really want to master. Anything I have learnt is all thanks to listening to the legends, in my case Sam Lovegrove and Allen Millyard, and it's just the most fantastic thing to learn anything at the venerable age of fifty-six.

While I've undeniably learnt quite a lot of basic mechanical stuff, I've probably learnt more in the way of what you might call 'decorative skills'. I've learnt how to distress things. I've learnt how to age things. I've learnt how to rattle-can stuff. I've learnt how to prime paint jobs. I've also learnt to approach things in a disciplined and rigorous order. So when you've got a rusty nut that won't come off, it's the wire brush you give it the once-over with firstly. Then try it. Don't work. So try a bit of penetrating oil. Leave it to soak in. That should work, but if it doesn't, apply heat with a blow lamp. And then give it a short, sharp knock, which can shock it into some kind of state to get it off. In the old days I'd have gone at it with the angle grinder.

That's how a shed changes you spiritually, physically and mentally. Physically just for obvious reasons, and hopefully ones that don't involve too many biscuits and do involve manual labour. But mentally and spiritually, the longer you are in a shed, I think the better the person you become. (As long as you don't pathologically hide away in it all the time. Solitude is great but you don't want loneliness in a shed, you know. So, you need to invite people in now and again.)

So there are many things that shed dwelling has taught me but towering above them all is patience. Before I started shed dwelling properly, I really thought I had a handle on the concept of patience, but actually, the reality of it is so different. One of the most special things about shed dwelling is that you have got to arm yourself with patience. And you know, why are you rushing to get these tasks done instead of luxuriating in the experience of doing them? There is a whole thing about this in Japanese culture, *wabi-sabi*, and it's about developing a worldview centred on the acceptance of transience and imperfection.

I feel like patience is part of that. If you're lucky enough to be replacing the head gasket on a Land Rover, then why are you rushing? Why aren't you enjoying every single moment of it? Don't rush. That's where mistakes happen – you rush rebuilding an engine and you find there are two sprocket washers left when you've finished. It happens, and it happens not so much because of a lack of talent but because of a lack of patience, the patience to check and double check that everything is good.

When you, on your own, have taken a carb off a Triumph T100, and you strip that carb, not quite knowing what to do, but you think you're learning, and then it goes *ping* all over the workbench, and you pick it all up but no matter how hard you try there is no denying that you've lost a really crucial spring . . . well, that's a real test of patience. There's so many times you just want to go, 'Stuff this for a game of soldiers, I'm going.' And maybe you do go for a little walk around the garden, but then you come back, you make yourself a cup of tea, and you find you have fresh eyes and you have another look for that spring. Maybe you find it, or maybe you find another one in your cubbyhole shelving that does the job, and you get the thing back together, and you put it back on the bike, and you give it a kick and, well, it still doesn't work.

When I first started shed dwelling, in that scenario, I started kicking the motorcycle and throwing spanners around, but if that happens to me now, I just go, 'Oh bollocks, that's shedding,' and I go and have another cup of tea, come back and look at it again. And then I say to myself, 'All right, I'm totally annoyed about it right now, but I'll strip it again and I'll enjoy the process again and maybe I'll learn something else; I'll learn what I did wrong last time.'

And that is a really good life indicator, I think. The tolerance of trying to find a spring and not finding it and having a mature reaction, to just take yourself away from the situation, have a cup of tea and come back.

The patience I've learnt in sheds has seeped into other areas of my life, such as rearing children. Let's say they're screaming and shouting and causing merry hell. Well, don't go absolutely mental with them. Just chill out, tell them where you're at, tell them what they should be doing and perhaps, you know, that kind of approach, which is a much more mellow one, works better than shouting and screaming and slamming doors. I've learnt that in a shed.

I've also learnt that there's no place for arrogance in a shed. No place for the show-off. Because being in a shed is classless. We're all the same in a shed really. There are people who we know are richer than us who come into the shed. There are people who have got a bigger collection than us who come into the shed, but actually, you know, you may be looking at an Alfa Romeo 8C worth ten million quid, but it boils down to the love and passion of engineering. That's why you're in the shed.

You're not in the shed to show off to someone but a shed does open the door on your soul, so, the people who you invite into your shed or who turn up to your shed looking for entry are not arrogant people on the whole. They're people who just want to celebrate and enjoy their passion with you, whatever that may be. And that again, you know, injects some kind of decorum and some kind of spiritual balance within a shed, and it is a shame, quite frankly, that such noble sentiments can't pervade other parts of society or life, you know what I mean? We're all on a level playing field in a shed. Your money's no good, your breeding's no good. But if you've got a passion for BSA Bantams, you're welcome in my shed anytime.

17:
Laugh Now, But Spend Enough Time in Sheds and You Too Will Surrender to the Genius of the Quilted Boiler Suit

I would urge every shed dweller to buy a quilted boiler suit. If you're short of heaters on a cold day, that's the cheapest way to keep warm in a shed. They're about thirty quid. I never realized they existed till I got involved in shed dwelling. They're like being in a sort of mobile duvet. They're fantastic. You feel like you're being held.

I think it's a big mistake not to have a hook with a boiler suit or two on it inside a shed. You really do want to make sure that what you're wearing is commensurate with what you're doing and a boiler suit is so handy for that. Also, a boiler suit is really safe if you're working with any kind of motorized tools because there's no straps or anything hanging out, and the moment you put it on you just feel about 25 per cent more competent. They were a big hit with women in munitions factories in the Second World War and, my sources in the fashion world tell me, are having a bit of a resurgence on the catwalk. But mate, for the shed, you definitely don't need one by Dolce & Gabbana. A quilted Snickers or Dickies boiler suit is probably the ultimate piece of shed wear for me.

You do also need to buy some Amblers work boots, the slip-on ones, with steel toecaps. The amount of stuff I've dropped on my toes is boundless, so, you need the steel toecaps to protect them, even if you don't have to contend with Sam Lovegrove treading on your foot for a laugh, which happens often to me. I say slip-on because once you're over forty, laces are for losers. The last thing you want to do is have to kneel down and unlace your boots to go into the house to go to the lavvy. You want to kick them off, mate. They want to be quick and easy to pull on and off. I live in the things. Don't get laces. That is confusing activity with progress.

Your trousers have got to be baggy in a shed, because there's a lot of bending down and leaning over and all that kind of stuff. Don't worry about showing your arse crack – worry about not getting your bollocks tied up in a tight pair of jeans. I mean, why would you wear tight clothing anyway? Because you think you look cool in it? You don't, mate. You're over forty. That's finished. So, you need some baggy jeans or work pants, ones that you don't care if a little bit of spillage goes on to them if you haven't got your boiler suit on in time.

Thick socks are an absolute corker and a must-have, because a lot of workspaces do, despite my aversion to it, have concrete floors. And you want a bit of cushion because it gets knackering being on a concrete floor, part of the reason why carpet is a top idea round your workbench, or some of those rubber mats. You don't want a concrete floor to work on. It really tires you out, standing on a hard floor. And when you kneel down to empty the oil out of the sump plug, you know, putting your knees on the concrete is horrible, speaking of which, I'm thinking I'm approaching the age of acquiring Velcro knee pads too. I go double sock from October, and rarely regret it.

So, the other thing that I'm really envious of, my mate Tony up in Preston, who's the chairman of the Cossack Owners' Club, he has braces. I really want braces. Braces are very much a shed dweller's accessory. I'm always envious of Guy, my mate, who wears braces. I'm very covetous of cool braces. Some people say you can't wear braces with jeans, that it just doesn't go. Nonsense. They're lovely. Deep red or tweed, preferably, with a nice old shirt with a warm Viyella kind of vibe to it.

A neck scarf I'm always very envious of. Everyone who's into steam has a little bandana round their neck. You've got to have some guts to wear that.

A cloth cap is an absolute go-to for the shed dweller, and you should always wear a hat. If you've got long hair (and hair is optional) an annoying thing is that when you lean forward, when you're fixing something or something like that, the hair goes over your eyes. So you need a cloth cap, a tweed cap, Fred Dibnah stylee. A hat is a critical thing.

One of the great things about a shed is that it doesn't

really matter what you look like. Shed dwellers are well used to not judging a book by its cover, and one of the results of that is that if you spend a lot of time in a shed you are likely to develop what is called 'shed hair'. Generally, shed dwellers whose follicles are still capable of producing keratin, have longer hair than your average human. Partly this is because a lot of us are actually counter-cultural at heart and don't like conforming, but also it's just that, you know, who wants to go and sit in the barber's when you could be reconditioning your window mechanism? When you're in a shed, one of the freedoms of the existence is that no one is ever going to tell you how you look.

Long hair, like mine, does have a pronounced practical disadvantage in that the hair goes over my face and eyes, so consequently I have to wear some kind of hat, or else put it in a pony tail, because obviously if I lean over a bike, I can't see anything. But the thing is that given the choice between wearing a hat and going to the barber's, I'd wear a hat any day of the week.

I like a cloth cap made out of good thick tweed. It keeps me warm and I think gentle heating on the head helps my brain work a little bit better, but I wouldn't go as far as sticking a hot water bottle under there. Because I wear my cloth cap the whole time, a lot of people think I'm bald underneath. But, honestly, it's just to stop the hair falling in my eyes, that's all. Generally speaking, while any headwear is more than very acceptable in a shed, the ubiquitous cloth cap is where it's at.

And with cloth caps you have a straight-up cloth cap,

like a farmer on *One Man and His Dog* in 1982, or you can go for a slightly more edgy baker boy cloth cap, which is my usual preference, which has pleated segments in it that look a bit like a cake. I think the baker boy hat is just a bit more stylish than the regular flat cap, but it's very much a question of personal choice.

I'm far too old to wear a baseball hat without looking like a wino. A good baseball hat on a younger person is often spot-on but be aware, wearer; baseball hats are cold in winter.

When I go to football I look around and everyone is wearing a baseball hat. I guess the baseball hat has replaced the cloth cap for football fans.

It's crucial to remember that while shed style is all about putting functionality over form, if you get it right, your wardrobe seamlessly correlates function and form together; in other words, if someone stops by the shed, you should like yourself, whatever that entails, whether, you know, you've got your favourite hoody on or a patchwork old tweed jacket with a crew neck jumper underneath.

Hoodies are insanely handy because they are so easy to slip in and out of, they're nice and warm if you buy a decent one, they hold your hair back (sort of) and you can, in an emergency, put the hood up and run to the house in a rainstorm when you need a wee and it's too wet to go outside.

I do also like, in principle, those warehouse smock coats. Only trouble is that in practice, your legs always come out from between the slit on the front of them, and you get oil on your knees or whatever it may be.

When you're getting involved in an engine, a head torch is really useful because you've still got both hands free so they are great in a shed when you are working with something really detailed. It's basically like an operating theatre, because if you want to do something really complex or intrinsic, and intimate, really tiny, then you need decent lighting, you know. I do like a magnifying glass on its own stand in a shed. That tells me that I am in the presence of someone who takes their shedding seriously. But day-to-day, a head torch is hard to beat. You get them for a tenner. They're really useful, and if you need to go for a pee, they are quite handy too. You can see it for a change, rather than just fumbling.

Now, when you're out and about, yeah, when you go into a jumble or something like that, I heartily recommend looking like rubbish. A torn wax jacket and dirty jeans, because you're probably holding folding when you're at a jumble, and if you look like shit, people don't think you've got much on you. If you're going out buying, you need to dress down a bit. Don't wear your three-piece tweed suit.

A good tip if you're selling is that you can always tell a man, as my mother used to say, by his shoes. So, if this guy is giving you a hard time over twenty quid, ignore his clothes and look at the shoes. If the geezer's got a Rolly on that means nothing. Could be a fake. But a pair of brogues? Well, you know, you might need to hold your nerve.

One thing I like about shed dwellers is that lots of them, like me, don't have any teeth. I do believe that if you're a proper shed dweller, you shouldn't worry too much about your teeth. I think it's okay not to have any teeth. I believe it smacks of someone being genuine, rather than a row of implants like an American news presenter. I think the lack of teeth shows an awful lot of confidence. The toothless don't give a shit. They're just into motorcycles, so why are you looking at me son, do you know what I mean? I do think that perhaps having the odd missing tooth is a badge of honour for shed dwellers.

When you see a geezer in the street, what is it about him that makes you think 'shed dweller'? Well, after oily hands, beards and thick socks comes the tool belt. They are interesting. Tool belts normally say: 'I have a building away from the house, of some description, where I spend much of my time.'

I'm gonna digress a bit here. 'What, again?!' Yes. So, right, chainsaws are very interesting for me. I have got one, but I've only used it about twice because you need the chainsaw trousers and all that kind of stuff.

But what I have discovered is that it's amazing how many things you think you need a chainsaw for, but actually, a good old hand saw will do it just as quick. If a big tree comes down and is blocking access to your shed, then you need a chainsaw, but you need a chainsaw with a blade the length of a fencepost, so, you know, leave it to the professionals. Chainsaws to me are quite scary. Funnily enough, I've got a 1940s chainsaw as a collection piece and that is terrifying. No guards, no nothing. How people have survived with both hands from the forties and fifties I've no idea.

Come to think of it, a lot of them didn't. A lot of them lost a finger or a thumb. It almost used to be a bit of a mark of respect, not to have all ten digits. I mean nine and a half, eight, you have a certain respect for them. It's not exactly a badge of honour but it's similar to how, as a biker, if you haven't broken your collarbone or shoulder, you haven't ridden motorcycles enough. I've broken my collarbone on one side, and I've broken my shoulder in three places on the other. And that's simply because I've ridden motorcycles for a very long time.

There are other badges of honour that shed dwellers acknowledge among each other, such as wearing steel boots to social occasions, the oily mark on the brim of your cloth cap where you've constantly pulled your hat down or rearranged it or pushed it up when you're looking at something – a great big oily mark under the brim.

18:
Of Mice and Men and the Sheds Wherein They Dwell

Let's talk about animals in sheds. When you've got a shed you're obviously going to share your world with some friends. And I do believe if you're a proper shed dweller, you should embrace, if not the whole animal kingdom, as much of it as won't chew through your wiring.

Now, the first thing that you really do need is a dog in a shed. A dog is the quintessential shed buddy. I'm just looking at my feral hound Jellybean right now, as it happens. You've got to have a dog in a shed. It's all part of shed life and being free. It's part of the joy of life, to have a dog that shares your shed with you, that has a little bed in the corner by the heater or by the wood burner. And it'll sit there quiet as a mouse, probably all day. When you obviously stop with your mates for tea and biscuits, it's got to have a little bit of biscuit, but it's someone you can talk to if you're working on your own. It's someone you can say to, 'What do you think about that, Jellybean?' And it can pass comment on the weld you've done with a little woof. I always find it's nice to have a dog to bounce ideas off, even though their ideas are sometimes a little hard to discern.

Dog-talk brings me on to the concept of a cat. Now, a cat's going to keep you relatively rodent-free but it's also going to keep you songbird-free. And the joy that I have in some of my sheds is that the sparrows are nesting in them, and blue tits and house martins and all that kind of stuff. And I think with a cat, you're actually running the risk of doing yourself over in having the worst of both worlds. But with a dog, it's not interested in slaying bird life, so consequently I think it's your all-round best companion.

But the absence of a cat does mean you may have an issue with vermin. I have to say I am quite partial to a mouse every so often. In fact, I used to have a pet one, years ago, like the bloke in *The Shawshank Redemption*. A field mouse with a little white chest. Now people say they pee and poop everywhere and all that kind of stuff and, okay they probably do, but we're in the shed here, so that's permitted.

But there isn't really much that good about rats. The biggest practical problem with rats is they eat wiring and all that kind of stuff, so they are absolutely a no-no. My mate Dave, who's a pest controller, he'll come around and for rats he'll leave out those bait boxes. Now, okay, the rat comes along, he eats the stuff and dies, but quite often he seems to die under the floorboards and then rot. Now people say that rats always go out to die and all that kind of caper, well, I've got to tell you it didn't work out that way for me. It stank the place out.

So, what I actually quite like the idea of doing now is getting the air rifle out. I could just sit there with the tea on and wait for Whiskers to show up. It's my shed, and if I want to fire a low-velocity weapon in it, having taken the relevant precautions, I'll do so. It's yet another reason to avoid concrete and metal sheds, you really don't want to let off a firearm in a container because of the ricochet, but if you have a wooden shed, what's the worst that's going to happen? You might blow a hole through the roof when you miss the rat, but that's no problem. You just will have to patch up the roof.

But you do need some sort of animal/insect/bird company in a shed. In one of my sheds there's a crack in the glass of one of the window panes and I've seen a Jenny wren go in there every so often. So, I'm thinking I'll keep the cracked window so she can get in and out still. Do you know what I mean? What's wrong with a little bit of poo on a Triumph? Clean it off and it's not a problem. I like a bit of wren poo to clean off, makes me feel useful.

Insects can be good, but I don't think they give as much feedback as a dog. I mean, there's a lot of insects that do share your shed with you like spiders and that kind of stuff, yeah? I do believe that spiders are a good thing to have in a shed but not too many. You need to keep abreast of the cobwebs, do you know what I mean? You can't be cobweb-ridden really, even though you feel that perhaps cobwebs are all right in a shed. I don't think they are. Unless there's one in a corner. When a great big wolf spider's in the corner up its funnel web, or whatever, then leave it.

19:
Tea

Shed dwellers have a special relationship with tea.

When you come into someone's house, you may well be offered a cup of tea or a cup of coffee. It's part of the welcoming process, a given, a prerequisite to anyone coming through the doors, tradesmen, carpet-fitters, even the guy delivering the new washing machine. In a shed, however, being offered a cup of tea is an invitation to stay, and not being offered one after, say, five minutes, is a pretty clear sign that the shed dweller would prefer it if you cleared off, sharpish.

I would go along with the adage that a shed is actually much more personal than your own home, because your own home, you share with people, generally, but your shed you don't. So it's the purest physical expression of you on the planet. Therefore, if you're asked whether you want a cup of tea in a shed, it signifies acceptance of you as a person that is liked.

In my experience, when you go into a house, you're also given the option of coffee. That don't happen in sheds as far as I'm concerned. I've never been offered a coffee in my life in a shed. If you go into a shed and someone says, 'Do you want a double espresso?' you'd be like, 'Hang on, what's this about? Who is this person? Does he dress strangely at the weekends?'

Now, the other issue with shed tea is that it has to be some variety of builder's. There's no room for Darjeeling or Earl Grey in a shed. It absolutely has to be builder's tea, because that's what you're expecting and that's the done thing. If someone offers you anything like green tea or chamomile, then you've got to question why they've got a shed.

Now, sheds are all about freedom and individuality so of course there are exceptions to these rules, one of which is Sam Lovegrove. Sammy is an official, dyed in the wool, approved hippy. Now Sam has what I call mung tea, and he spends almost as much time in the shed creating his tea as he spends creating the most wonderful motorcycles. I'm not joking. He will spend a very long time measuring out the right mung to mix with the other mung. I've no idea what goes into his tea, but if he's feeling excitable, he will have some honey with it. (And that's an interesting thing as well. More and more, I get offered honey in my tea these days, even in sheds.)

So, Sammy has his herbal teas, but you do not generally go into a shed of any credibility that has an array of herbal teas in a little display cabinet. Right? It's just tea bags, son. You know? Not loose tea. Is there a reason to have loose tea in a shed? I don't think so. Unless you're Sam Lovegrove and you want some special mung mix, if you see what I mean. But, globally, the tea bag has taken over. Loose tea would be amazing if it worked, the little grippy thing, the little ball thing that you flip. It's such a cool bit of technology but it just doesn't work. We don't really have time for it. We probably could but it's much better just to have the bag. I think loose-leaf tea is for ponces at the weekends to be honest. I imagine people in Islington brewing a pot on their wooden kitchen table, just taking it off the Aga.

The heating of water in a shed normally takes place in a pretty rancid kettle, although in rural Cornwall, on the odd occasion, someone will put the gas stove on to boil the water out of a saucepan. Saucepan tea is not ideal, but it's way better than a cup of tea made with hot water out of one of those taps that people have in their houses. I do not like them. I don't understand where it comes from for one thing. All I do know is that they absolutely terrify me.

You put the tea bag in, and you hit the outer ring three or four times, up and down and then twist it and BOOSH, out comes the boiling water and it's spitting and frothing and steaming up my glasses and I cannot see what I'm doing. You need two hands to deal with it, one to hold down the ring and the second one to hold the mug, so your glasses steam up, you can't take them off and you burn your hands. Every time I have used one of them that happens. I've tried taking my glasses off but then I can't see anything.

Nothing beats a kettle, let's be honest. It's the whole ritual of the kettle, right? You put the water in, you have a look in it every so often, there's an awful lot of limescale in there but that'll be okay, I'll swish that out next time. You boil it, it's done, you get a cup of tea.

There's something missing from the ritual when you use a hot tap. Plus, I mean, do we really have to be in such a hurry in our lives that we can't boil a kettle? We've got to spend thousands of pounds on a tap that gives us hot water? What's happened? The march of the hot tap is confusing activity with progress; spiritually, physically and mentally. You don't need to do that! Life ain't got to be that quick. We're told that we've got to chill out but actually, everyone is trying to make us live life faster and faster to the extent where people can't even be patient enough to let a kettle boil.

I tell you, waiting for that kettle to boil, in the home or the shed, that's emotionally stabilizing you of a morning. This hot tap movement, immediately you're in it, straightaway. Boiling water, steam, third-degree burns; it's just a nightmare. You have got to take it easy, man, in the morning. Even if you're getting up at four to go to work, it's still worth waiting for the kettle to boil, son. Get up ten minutes earlier and wait for the kettle, it's a very good spiritual discipline.

When I'm away I have this electric coil thing that I can stick in a mug and boil the water in it. They're probably not legal any more.

Tea is not just about caffeine. Its purpose is to provide a pause button in life, and the boiling of the kettle is part of that. Tea/life is actually about stopping and taking it all in, whether for good or bad, whether there's commiserations to be had or excitement to celebrate. The cup of tea is something, without which, life wouldn't be worth living.

I was a smoker for forty years and one of the great joys of my life was saying, 'Stuff this, let's go and have a fag.' I can't do that at fifty-six, because I will die from it, but there is nothing better in my world – and I really would genuinely say nothing better, sex ain't better, going on holiday to the Caribbean ain't better, taking Jennifer Aniston out to dinner ain't better – than a cup of tea and a vape with a mate. And if it's in a shed, your shed, where you're content and at peace, well, that's the Holy Grail, isn't it? You've done it.

Would you believe it, my wife's just brought me a cup of tea. Just this moment. Just as I am sitting here writing this. That is like her basically booking me some flights for a romantic weekend in Venice – but cheaper. She's basically saying to me, 'Henry, even though you are a twat, I love you.'

Colour-wise, shed tea for me has to be beige. I don't want any cream or ivory white nonsense, you know? I don't want it swimming in milk. I want my tea beige. Not brown. Beige. I want beige. Dark beige, maybe, but no darker than a dark beige Marks & Spencer's V-neck jumper, if you know what I mean. It's interesting because while I do like it strong, I don't like it like conker-coloured. As my mate Tommy says, 'Just a splash of milk.' Now, Tom is a very, very good tea drinker, as you often find with people who have done quite a bit of sitting around in sheds in their lives, and there is a lot of wisdom and lived experience in that milk-quantity specification.

I'm a bit of a neat freak in my shed, so one thing I really hate is when someone makes a new cup of tea without clearing the old one away first. Before you know it, you're racking up the cups, and that's why in most sheds I think the two-cup protocol (TCP) is an appropriate mess-minimization measure.

The TCP dictates that you only have two cups in the shed; one is yours, which just goes round and round with a hot water slosh serving to clean and warm it between beverages, and the spare is for guests. Store them turned upside down so no little woodland insects make a home in them.

That hot water sterilization thing is very important actually. Too often you're given a cup of tea in a shed that, obviously, all that was done was that it was swilled out with cold water very quickly. This really is a no-no in this day and age. Guests are entitled to a clean cup, one which has seen some hot water since its last usage. Rinsed out with boiling water, given a quick whizz round, is fine by me as long as it doesn't have those stains round the lip of the mug, the lips slobber chop stains. I don't mind the odd spider and that kind of stuff. That's not an issue. But really, you know, you need to be careful sometimes in some people's sheds. People will understand if the actual main body of the mug has a bit of oil on it or something. That's all right. But where you put your lips, darling, that's got to be clean really. Or at least appear to be clean.

There is no excuse for having terrible mugs in a shed these days, because if you go to a country fair, people are giving away mugs. You need to go round with a carrier bag and get all the freebie mugs and bring them back. If I'm going to the Bristol Car Show, then there might be free mugs, so I'll bring my carrier bag. Failing that, second-hand mugs from a second-hand shop (usually collected from the Bristol Car Show in the first place, by the way) are 10p. There's no excuse to have chipped mugs.

As I believe I may have mentioned heretofore, I like fixing stuff, but fixing mugs is a mug's game. I'm ruthless with them; if there is a chip, it's gone. Stains are fine but if it's chipped, get down to somewhere that's giving away free mugs.

It's tricky when the handle breaks off a beloved mug. Gluing it back together if the handle drops off is understandable, I feel your pain, but at the same time, you must understand that one day it's going to fall in your lap. It'll go again. It's the threat of lap burn that stops me doing that. You'll just be painting something and having a sip of tea and the handle will drop off and it will go everywhere, and you just don't need that in your life. So while it's nice to picture yourself gluing the handle back on, don't think, 'Oh, I've saved another one,' because actually, no, you've not, you've just delayed the outcome.

Needless to say, I've never been into a shed and been offered tea with a saucer and a cup. I've also never, ever had a plate in a shed. Plates are for the house. If you get a doughnut or a biscuit, you're supposed to just hold it with the mug of tea, in my view. Anything that turns up on a plate is suspicious in a shed.

When it comes to kettles, the ritual of making tea in the shed is often dictated by the location of the kettle. The shed owner says: 'Henry, mate, do you want a cuppa?' I go, 'Yeah, that would be nice, mate.' He goes, 'Do you want any sugar?' I go, 'No, son, it's fine, right.' So, that in itself is a sort of dialogue transaction that happens the nation over.

But where is the kettle located? This is critical. If the kettle is actually in the house, that means that you are left in the shed on your own, so, consequently people will delay offering tea until they feel comfortable that you can be in the shed on your own and not have an accident with the air compressor or lift their prized collection of RAC badges. So, if after ten minutes, you're not being offered tea, it means that the kettle's in the house and the geezer thinks you're a counter-jumper and you should probably leave. Now, if you're a mate on a return visit to the shed, then etiquette dictates that you can probably go with the shed owner to the kitchen to chat while the tea is being made. That means you're totally in. You are a proper paid-up member of that shed. You're approved. If, on the other hand, the tea is actually made on site in the shed, then the offer of tea will come relatively quickly because the geezer can keep an eye on you.

Tea in sheds is a bit like how when people talk about the weather, they're not really talking about the weather, are they? They're getting to know each other. And we do also make judgements about people based on what kind of tea they ask for. I mean, if someone asks for no milk, that's suspicious. I sometimes think they think they're a bit better than me. (Unless it is in the context of, 'Oh, sorry, Henry, I haven't been down the shop yet, are you all right with it black?' You get that quite a lot too.)

If they go, 'Milk and two sugars,' you know they're genuine, although nowadays you can go, 'No sugar,' and that won't offend anyone.

It's been a while since I had anyone ask for three or even four sugars, to be honest, and I do think anything over two sugars is a little bit fishy these days. It's almost like they're getting a meal out of you. There used to be a lot of four-sugars lads in the seventies and eighties, and I'd guess they're all dead, because if you're having four sugars in a cup of tea, then what on earth does dinner look like?

'Have you got any sweetener?' is definitely beyond the pale. You might as well ask the geezer to leave there and then. I've only seen people bring out their own sweetener twice in forty years of sheddery. I think it's detrimental to the interactive nature of a shed.

Leaving the bag in is wrong, I think. It affects the taste and deprives the cuppa of its elegance, not to mention falling on your face when you drain the cup, not knowing it's hiding down there. Modern tea bags dissipate their flavour very quickly, so there's no real need to leave the tea bag in anyway.

I do think the tea bag should be disposed of properly, as well, either in a designated bowl/soapdish or else in the bin. If you get someone to make the tea for you, and they leave the tea bag on the side, just by the sink, that's like insulting to my dignity. I want the tea bag properly disposed of. I want it in the bin. I don't want it left in the sink or on the draining board, because otherwise, after you've gone and I've had a nice afternoon, I suddenly see this turd on my draining board, and I think, 'What kind of a person can do that? I sold him that bike way too cheap!' So, do what you want in your own shed, of course, but never leave a tea bag on a draining board in another man's shed.

In the old days, people used to put the same tea bag back in the cup for a second go-round, and give it another squeeze. I've never actually put it on the discard pile and then returned it to a cup two hours later, but I have motivated myself to make up to three cups of tea with one bag simultaneously, when there were no bags left, and I just had the one. To be honest, a modern tea bag will easily do two mugs, but I was at someone's shed the other day and they put two tea bags in one cup. It was definitely wrong, and proof that people are deranged although, weirdly, it was an amazing cuppa and, as I say, your shed is your castle.

Powdered, condensed and evaporated milks all have their place. My dear parents-in-law, they love a bit of powdered milk in their coffee because there is a certain taste to it, and I was brought up on condensed milk, Carnation and strawberries, so I also quite like condensed milk in moderation. I think condensed milk in a shed is fine if the shed is a huge distance from the house. I can also cope with UHT milk. It's theoretically a very nice resource to have in the shed, but I've never, ever been confronted by one of those little plastic containers outside a hotel room. UHT could serve a purpose in a shed, but I would say it's a little bit too complex for a lot of shed dwellers to go and acquire.

At the luxurious end of shedding, you get a fridge and in the fridge is a pint of milk. I would strongly urge anyone thinking of acquiring a shed fridge not to be lured by the siren call of the mini fridge. I would just like to give you a health warning with mini fridges, because I've tried them in sheds, and they don't last very long for some reason. I've had two or three and after about three months of refrigerating, they seem to give up, just when the milk is most needed, so I would advise against buying a mini fridge. To repeat: mini fridges: avoid.

Perhaps the ultimate mark of acceptance is when you're going to see your mate's shed, and he says, 'Do you want a cup of tea, Henry? I've just made this Thermos.' Because if you've got two little cups of a Thermos to share, you might as well be married. That is more intimate than sex in my view. I do find it weird that when I was younger I would have gone to a party and had sex with somebody I had literally just met and these days I wouldn't let them into my shed on that basis. I mean, I am pretty sure they probably wouldn't be interested in coming into my shed anyway, but even if they were I'd only let someone in the shed after the third year of dating, probably.

I love the Thermos, but I hate those hot mug things. I see them a lot in petrol stations, and I think, 'Ooh, should I buy one?' But then, you see, I think they're synonymous with people who climb mountains and wear branded fleeces – which is fine, but it isn't me. So, I've never actually bought one, and when I've been given one I've found that the tea is actually too hot to drink and it tastes metallic. There's often a little spout at the top that the tea comes shooting out of, burns your lips and dribbles down your white t-shirt.

I mean the joy of a mug is that it cools predictably so you can pick your own heat levels. But it cools pretty quick. You can't hang around with a cup of tea. It's a seven-minute window, I reckon, and that timeframe is an important element of the tea break. You see, when you're working in a shed, a cup of tea is not just a cup of tea, it's a break. It's an opportunity to stop your work and review what you're up to. It's also an opportunity to take in your surroundings.

And most importantly, it's something to do when you've broken something, and made a mistake. Right? So, you think, ah, damn, I've just dropped four bolts into the engine. I'm going to go have a cup of tea. So, you have a cup of tea and you come back and you look at the engine and you look at how you can get those nuts out of the engine. So how to placate yourself for being such a wazzock is all about stopping and having the tea.

If you're lucky enough to be young enough to still be able to smoke without any guilt, then that's the ultimate tea break, but for me it has to be a vape and a cup of tea.

But the coming of the tea imposes its own time limit on this reflection period, and that time limit is dictated by the heat of the tea, and this is why I've got issues with those hot mugs and things, because a good old mug of tea only lasts seven minutes and then you knock it all back in one go, and think, either, 'Right, I'm going to give it a go.' Or, 'Nah, I'm done for today.' It's a time-limited window of inaction to reflect either on the satisfaction that you've managed to do something, or that you're a wazzock.

One thing I hate is when you have a tea break in the shed and the mobile phone rings. It completely wrecks your tea break buzz. You set yourself up and go, right, I'm just going to get this front end in on the bike and then I'll have a cup of scorch. And then you go off to the house, make the tea, come back to the shed and the phone rings, and it's your partner saying, 'You know you've got to be watching the kids at five o'clock this afternoon playing basketball?' 'Have I? Oh!' And then you get into a big discussion about non-shed related issues and when you hang up the tea is cold.

Cold tea should be thrown away, I think. Some people say you can microwave it but I don't know. I would rather throw the tea away and go and make a fresh one but in part that's because I'm always constantly suspicious of milk. Also, who has a microwave in a shed?

The major criminal act where tea is concerned is leaving a full cup of tea to go cold in the shed overnight, and then you come in and see it in the morning, with the kind of oil slick on top, and that's nearly murder in my view. I mean, that is appalling behaviour. Can you imagine doing that to your shed? Sacrilege, innit? It's weird how much harder it is to clean a mug that's had tea in it that's gone cold. It's got that kind of rim round it, that adherence. It coagulates most unpleasantly.

To be honest, there's not much to be gained in putting a cup of tea down. If you make yourself a tea and you have a couple of sips of it and then you put the tea down, the chances are you'll get distracted. And then, when you come back to the tea it's lukewarm, and where is the fun in that? I think it's better to identify while having the tea what you're going to do next. Enjoy your tea, finish it, put down the empty mug and then hit it.

I am lucky I suppose in that I will drink, and enjoy, tepid

tea. The limit is where a biscuit doesn't go slightly squidgy when you dunk it. That is the litmus test: when you dunk a Ginger Nut in it and the Ginger Nut doesn't soften, in the dunking timeframe. Normally it's dunk, take out, munch, but if it tastes cold on the biscuit, you have got to get rid of the tea. There's no point carrying on.

Some people get very anxious when, for one reason or another, they can't get to their usual shop, so they go up to the Spar or whatever, and they buy a packet of tea bags and they bring them back and they're saying the tea they produce is like dishwater but they've bought 160 of them. Now, I think they're barking up the wrong carrot here. Because when you go down the local shop and you buy builder's tea and you get it home and you are not happy with the resulting liquid, the problem is not about the bag. Let's be clear on this. Every manufacturer nowadays in the UK makes a good tea bag, in my experience.

The problem is with the person who's making it. Now, there are some golden rules on tea making in a shed. The first one is, don't hang around. Some people put the tea bag in, bung the boiling water in and leave it for fifteen minutes to brew. Well, that destroys the tea, because what happens is the scum from the kettle collates over the surface of the hot water, so you put the milk in and there's dark patches and light patches across the top. This is wrong.

We're in the twenty-first century and the technology that's gone into tea bags is tip-top. So, you lob the tea bag in, you put the boiling water on top of it, and you try and aim, when you're pouring the water, to hit the tea rather than just the corner of the bag, right? You then bring it up to the level you need. You get the teaspoon in, you whizz it around and squidge it a bit and it's done, man. Take the bag out, lob it in the bin, not on the side as previously discussed, a little bit of milk to taste and you are done. None of this, 'Oh, I'm going to let it brew.'

And you really don't need a teapot. Unless you're Sammy, obviously.

20:
Biscuits

You don't, of course, have to have a biscuit every time you have a cup of tea, especially if you suffer from finish-the-packetitis, like me, but a shed with no biscuits in it is a pretty morose place.

Now, of course, when you are talking about shed biscuits, you kind of have to start with a wide-ranging discussion of the Hobnob. The Hobnob portrayed itself as the first journeyman biscuit that had the courage to say, 'I can be something special,' but, I want to get one thing out there right away. I'm not a Hobnob fan. I know it's a crazy thing for a shed dweller like me to say, and I do want to make one thing absolutely clear, which is that I will eat any biscuit that is given to me or offered to me, right, including a Hobnob, so, this isn't about me chucking my toys out of the pram and saying, 'I won't eat one of those.' I will, but there are preferences, and probably at number 142 in my personal top biscuit rundown, you'd find Hobnobs. Mainly because I find them too salty for my palate. It's probably only me, but I feel as though I'm eating a coronary in a packet.

But, look, I hate to talk negatively about any biscuits, so let's start with what is, in my humble opinion, the greatest biscuit of all time: the plain digestive with no chocolate. Its key attribute is its oaty goodness and it's an iconic biscuit for dunking, just the right consistency. I insist my digestives have to be McVitie's, in the red packet because the rest of them, the knockoffs, are all inedible, like chewing on sawdust.

Next up, Bourbon biscuits. Legends in their own lunchtime, and divine to dunk because the biscuit itself is just the right consistency to go a little bit soft on the dunk, while basically still somehow staying hard, and, get this, the chocolate filling remains slightly cool. Now obviously, if you dunk for too long, like over one and a quarter seconds, then you've got a problem with any biscuit and I do recommend having some utensil near at hand to fish out any dunk-detritus. (Don't use a screwdriver. A screwdriver's obviously useless for getting soluble bits of biscuit out.) So it's dunk, take a beat, eat, and that basically results in the warm sensual feeling on the outside yet on the inside the chocolate bit is still slightly cool. That's biscuit bliss in my book.

I think that the genius of the Bourbon is that the paste in the middle that holds the two planes of the biscuit together bestows incredible rigidity on the finger compared to the regular biscuit. They simply don't break. They can chip around the sides, sometimes an entire panel can fall off, but the chances of a Bourbon accidentally snapping are so statistically negligible as to be equivalent to zero.

Peek Freans are incredible strivers for excellence. They should be knighted those people. I hope they've been given the Queen's Award for Industry.

Now, third, I come back once again to the McVitie's

Digestives, but this time with either milk or plain chocolate coating. Fabulous dunking potential. The brilliant thing about the plain chocolate is that they're not quite as moreish as the milk chocolate, so you go through them a bit slower. Also, people under the age of thirty-five don't like dark chocolate which is fantastic when it comes to protecting your hoard against unauthorized intruders (e.g. sprogs) in search of chocolatey, gluten-based snacks. (Just on a side note, a square of pure chocolate, half-eaten with the cup of tea to melt it in the mouth is pretty good too, but chocolate is very much for the house not for the shed, just in my opinion.)

Now, sorry to be hating again, but custard creams to me are way overrated, although you must refer back to what I said in the first place which is I'll eat any biscuit. On a cold day in a shed in Cumbria, if someone offers you a custard cream, you're going to eat the packet. Now, some people say that the elegant decorative gothic and Romanesque features adorning a custard cream are to be admired, but these fripperies are inconsequential to me. It's all about the taste. I can understand why the etching and engraving on the biscuit casing is something to probably look at and even rejoice in briefly, when you have the first one of the day, or while you admire your biscuit in advance of eating it, but by the time you are having your eighth custard cream I think you have to take a sterner view on issues like that.

The little nutty biscuit that you sometimes get in a packet with a cup of coffee in a hotel with pretensions is an interesting beast. I call them Lotus biscuits and they are one of my favourites.

Now, let's talk about Ginger Nuts. As well as being a limit-less seam of double entendre jokes, I will always have a deep emotional attachment to this workhorse of the biscuit world because for my old man, bless him, his favourite biscuit hack was to leave the Ginger Nuts out for a couple of days, so they went bendy. Now, with all this health and safety guff I think they're made differently, so you can't leave them out and make them bendy; if you leave them out they just disintegrate and get sort of crumbly. But back in the day in the seventies and eighties, the Ginger Nut would bend and it would become slightly chewy and that was unbelievably exciting in what was an otherwise bleak era for biscuitology.

They're stalwarts for dunking, and they are absolutely suited to shed dwellers because they don't seem to be affected by the wild variations of temperature in a shed either. They're just as nice at 30°C, or minus three. They don't seem to worry about that, something to do with their consistency. They're also a valuable constituent of the biscuit arsenal because they're vegan and, believe it or not, there are increasing numbers of vegan shed dwellers, and, for me, if everyone in the shed has got biscuit bonhomie, that really lends itself to a good day in the shed.

When I rode Route 66 for *World's Greatest Motorcycle Rides* I bought a massive family pack box of Oreo biscuits for the road. I won't have anything else in America because not only are you riding the American Dream, you're eating it as well. It's an all-encompassing experience. It would be sacrilege to have a quintessential British biscuit like a digestive on Route 66. I mean, when in Rome and all that.

I'm only interested in the original Oreo biscuit. Once you get into all the other variants that they created, they can clear off. It's got to be the original Oreo biscuit or nothing. And nothing is heinous. So, you've got to go original. Also, you're supposed to dunk them in milk. But that's wrong. You don't want to do that. What would you dunk it in milk for? That's so Spielberg, circa 1983.

So, those are my top everyday biscuits, but then there is the whole world of posh biscuits; there's a Viennese finger (two shortbreads with some chocolate in the middle), stunning, gorgeous, but they're for special occasions.

Straddling the two worlds is the Maryland chocolate chip cookie. You see, Marks & Spencer's, all these people, they do these very posh chocolate chip cookies which are totally edible, but the Maryland cookie's cheap, cheerful and accessible to everybody. They dunk beautifully and they're just the right smallness, so you can have ten and think that you've only really had a couple. You can't have ten Marks & Spencer's special luxury chocolate chip cookies. You feel really guilty because they're in those kind of plastic segments where you take them out, and you can't help but look at those empty slots and go, 'Have I had six?' But with Marylands, there's just a tube of biscuits so you can have half the packet and then think, 'Ah, they're only small.' And walk off.

It wouldn't be right not to give anything but an honourable mention to Cadbury's work in improving biscuit landscape. The mini roll and the chocolate finger stand out, but keep your white chocolate fingers away from me please.

There's also the biscuit for an actual celebration, you

know, when you finally got that headlight rewired and I would put the Boaster in that category. They're the original luxury biscuit, I think, the Boaster, they kind of invented the category. I've never been partial to a Wagon Wheel myself, but I must try a bit harder with them, but I tell you what, at Christmas in the shed, may I suggest a Tunnock's Teacake? Oh I may, I may. A Tunnock's Teacake is for 'I've just finished a restoration.' A Tunnock's Teacake says: 'Those parts have just arrived that I've been waiting for for years.' Tunnock's is the king. I wouldn't ever go more than two, though, or you're going to feel queasy.

If you're talking Tunnock's, as we are, then we can't really talk about their teacake without talking about their caramel wafer, which is a delight, and neatly segues us into unwrapping individual biscuits; and then we're in a whole different world. Because if you've got the caramel wafer, then you've got the Club and you've got the Penguin which obviously is a dyed in the wool favourite over years and years. And the Club biscuit. I mean, wow. The way they snap. The orange Clubs are my favourite but fill your boots with the raisin and mint.

Those biscuits traverse the ever-closing gulf between the bar and the biscuit. They're the perfect compromise, because, you see, I don't think you can really go full Crunchie/Twirl/ Flake in the shed. They don't really go with tea. And crisps are anathema as well for me. I had a terrible experience with those bacon Wheat Crunchies once, which just returned every twenty minutes. You can't have that. Not in a shed.

21:
Why You Should Never, Ever Buy Anything at an Auction But Almost Certainly Will

Obtaining booty to take back to the shed is vital, and often involves attending auctions. The buyers at vehicle auctions are uniquely of the male species. It's all men. There are women there – about six of them behind the desk telling all the men where to go, what to do and when the next lot's coming up.

I've got to say, when I walk into an auction, I experience a flashback to the emotions that I used to get when I was going to a party at the age of nineteen and was hoping that girl I really fancied was going to be there: massive excitement combined with an equal and opposite fear that I'm going to blow it, and a soupçon of nausea for good measure. You have the same feeling when you walk into an auction.

You are constantly in a battle against what they call 'auction fever', which is when you lose the run of yourself and buy stuff that you have to hide from your wife. It's a hard thing to avoid contracting, however, because as you go round and look at stuff, you find yourself pondering the purchase of items you wouldn't even look at if they were in a shop with a price tag on them. But, you see an old rusted-out cab of a tractor and you note it down in the catalogue when you're wandering around. 'Could be a possible, max eighty quid.' You know damn well you don't really want it, but at the same time you want to be part of the auction and you never know, most importantly, you might just get the unbelievable bargain of the century.

Now, you have to be aware that there's probably more chance of being involved in a lethal accident involving a clothes peg than there is of getting a genuine result in an auction that is a proper cheap deal, but once you know that, it's a great day out. Of course, people persist and they think, 'Man, I've got a really good deal at an auction.' Well, there's a reason for that. It comes with no warranty. The person who's selling it to you is faceless; they've gone with your money. They've left. And you're left with this total rust bucket. If you want to get collectibles and restoration projects, then an auction is fine, but don't go for a car you want to drive every day. It's a much better idea to go to a shop because then you've got some comeback.

One classic mistake is to bid too early, but the other is to wait too late. Let's say, for example, that there are three CX500 motorcycles, all identical, dotted throughout the sale, one at the beginning, one in the middle, one at the end. Now, if you go for the first one, the second one will sell cheaper, that's guaranteed. So you cleverly decide to wait for the third one, because it's a little bit shabby and you reckon the first and the second ones will weed out all the bidders. But then the third one comes up and it's the last opportunity to get one, so the bidding goes crazy and if you do get it, you pay more than you would have for the first or the second ones which were better.

Really, the important thing to remember is that there is no way to win at auction. Once you've got that straight, it's a blast. It's all about the craic. It's all about the sausage and egg sandwiches and eating white bread without your wife giving you shit. I never go to the viewing the day before. I turn up a few hours early, get myself a bacon butty and have a whizz round before the bidding starts.

It's pure excitement, and although you mustn't get into this auction fever thing, you will. It's proper exciting because you're having a bid on stuff, but you're not quite getting anything, and then suddenly this Morris Minor comes up and you think, 'I'll have a go on it' and you end up buying it! Now, the second before the guy shouts 'Sold' and points at you, that's probably the high point of this whole procedure. Because within seconds you'll be wondering, 'What have I done?' Then, you pay in the office and go back out to pick it up and as you load it onto the trailer you realize you have just bought a Morris Minor on which, basically, the entire subframe is totally shot, the chassis is rusted through and the steering wheel is hanging off the dash by a thread. It's like eating a massive chocolate cake in one go, fun at the time but liable to lead to indigestion.

And as you drive home, thinking over how you wanted a Harley and are coming back with a Morris Minor four lots down, the best option is to turn around and go back to the auction house and beg them to take it off your hands because you are going to get major purchase-depression when you get back to the shed and you take that hunk of junk off the trailer and the wheels fall off. That is the exact moment you will realize why it went into an auction in the first place.

My view is that you use auctions for collectibles for the shed. A petrol pump, or a tin can, or a sign or some cubbyhole shelving. That way, the only thing to worry about is; is it genuine? That's your only worry. If you're buying a vehicle that you want to use every day, an auction is not the place to buy. People put everyday vehicles into auction precisely because they're knackered. If you genuinely believe you're going to take a car out of an auction, turn on the ignition and it's going to drive forever, like you're buying a new car or something, then you're deluded.

If, on the other hand, you are looking for a restoration project and you know that you're buying, let's say, a beach buggy for five grand, and you know that beach buggy is going to need another four grand of parts on it and six months in the shed, and you understand that, then auctions are the best fun places to be on the planet.

The other point is – don't forget about the commission – and the VAT on the commission! It can range from anything from 2–30 per cent.

That's why I've got to say, the way to get deals is to drink tea, man. Get in a shed, drink tea with the geezer and ask: 'How much do you want for the Morris Minor?' 'Oh, you don't want that Henry, she's useless, why don't you try that Fiat over there, mate, she's all right, quite solid.' They know that you know where they live.

The whole scam used to be: you buy at auction, do it up and then flog it. Now, you buy it from a shed, do it up and flog it at auction. It's round the other way. I think it's because over the last couple of years, people, the DFLs – the Down from Londons – go along to the auction thinking, 'Oh, darling, let's go and buy ourselves a Spitfire', so you're going to pay through the nose for it cos it's not just trade any more. So, approach an auction with care, stick to your limit, accept there is a high chance that anything electrical won't work – and you'll be okay.

Another interesting observation I have made over the years is that if you're going to a general auction, let's say of tractors, then the prices are going to be lower than if you go to a dispersal auction of, let's say, Henry Cole's collection. Reason being, that if the person is well-known within, say, the tractor heritage industry or whatever, they are going to command probably 20 to 30 per cent more on a lot of items. Because people go, 'Oh, it was owned by Henry, must be a bloody good one.' Well, they're right, it is a good one. If you're going to buy my 135 Massey, it's a peach and you wouldn't expect anything less from a man of my calibre, obviously. So, that tractor is worth seven grand, when at a general sale you'd probably get it for three and a half, four tops.

It's important, I think, at auctions, to try and imagine how you will feel on the journey home, and to role play in your head the moment when you park up and your partner comes out of the house and goes, 'How did it go?'

SCENARIO A:

You gesture forlornly at the empty trailer. She smiles and says: 'Didn't you get it then?' 'No. I didn't. The price was wrong.' And she goes, 'Oh, darling, bad luck!' 'I know. It just went for so much money, I'm absolutely gutted.' 'Oh, do you want a cup of tea?' 'Oh, please.'

And then she'll make it, not you, which is good. Now you've got an amazing opportunity, as you're sitting there in the kitchen looking sad, to go, 'The really annoying thing is I'm now going to have to go to these other two auctions with my mates, because they know more than I do about it,' which is obviously a load of bollocks, and although you've come back technically empty-handed, because you haven't got the motorbike you said you were going to get, what she doesn't know is that you got a couple of tin signs and a couple of oil cans that are in the side pocket of the driver's door, which obviously get sneaked into the shed at a later date.

So, I would think there is nothing to be guilty of or embarrassed about by coming back from an auction empty-handed. It can work in your favour, always remember that, because it gives you a pink ticket for looking depressed and hard done by and therefore allows you to go to other auctions, on other weekends. It gives the appearance of responsibility, and if you're lucky, you might get an overnight with the lads. Otherwise you have to make up spurious shit, like, 'I'm going to this auction because I think there's some mudguards for the bike I bought,' and you soon run out of components.

Then, there's the three other scenarios when you *have* unloaded the contents of your wallet at auction.

SCENARIO B:

'Hello darling, did you have a nice time at the auction?' 'Well, I bought something,' you say. 'Have you? What?' So, you go round and open the doors. Now you've got to be absolutely sure of yourself in what you've bought, you've got to be on your mettle. And she says, 'Oh, darling, is that the Bantam D1? You've been looking for one of those for years. Did you get it cheap?' 'Yes, darling, I did. 600 quid.' 'God, that's amazing. Cup of tea?'

SCENARIO C:

'Hello darling, did you have a nice time at the auction?' 'Well, I bought something.' 'Have you? What?' So, you go round and open the doors. And she says, 'Oh, darling, is that the Bantam D1? You've been looking for one of those for years. Did you get it cheap?' You suck in some breath. 'Well, I did pay a little bit over the odds, because I got carried away.' 'Did you? How much?' '1,250 quid.' (Actually it was £1,600 when you include the commission.) '1,250 quid, for that piece of junk? Have you lost your mind? What about my new kitchen?'

SCENARIO D:

You are lurking in your van at the end of your road. You see your missus pulling out to go to the shops. You race in, park, wheel an absolute disaster of a D1 off the trailer, the exhaust hanging off it, the mudguards rattling, oil dripping out of every component. Looking anxiously over your shoulder, you wheel it round into the shed. Your wife gets back from the shop and leans out the window. 'Hello darling, did you have a nice time at the auction? Get anything?' 'Nope.' You are now basically having an affair with a piece of machinery. That's why, when you go to an auction you need to visualize yourself coming home from the auction.

22:
Staying Alive, With a Little Help From Your Shed

I was sitting in a shed the other day when my mate Chris starts talking about his prostate. He's been for the blood test and his PSA count was way up in the sky so, you know, it's finger up the bum time on the next visit and he's kind of nervous about it. He's seventy, but he's an old boy in his soul, and he says he's thinking about not going. Then Mick is like, 'Chris, don't be daft son. I had it done. It's fine. Bit cold with the jelly and that, but you've got to do it.' It did strike me that the only place that a man's going to talk about stuff like that with other men is in a shed. So anyway, Chris pulls his cap down and says he'll do it.

I saw him a few weeks later and, although I didn't ask, he comes right out with it. 'Guess what Henry! I had it done. Finger up the bum. Lady doctor too. She didn't even blink.' 'That's great, son. What's the prognosis?' I say. 'Not great but not terrible. I mean, I've got prostate cancer, but she said lots of men my age have, and it's slow moving enough they might not even do anything, you know, because something else will get me first.' 'Holy smoke, Chris. You've got cancer!

That's terrible.' 'No, I know it seems that way Henry, but it's not. The lady doctor explained it all to me. It's not exactly benign but it doesn't matter. They can give me something to slow it down as well if the PSA goes up any more.'

I think there is a better understanding now of how difficult it is for men with mental or physical problems to actually talk about it with our mates. Now for these younger men, it's much easier than it is for us old farts, because they have been brought up doing it, and even they find it hard, despite the fact they've got the Prince Williams of this world making them aware that they should talk about mental health etc. And quite rightly so, good luck your highness, keep it coming, but don't forget that men also need a nice cosy physical place to talk about their problems.

The bottom line is that if you've got an inflamed prostate, a wart on the end of your knob or you feel like killing yourself because you got PTSD from a car crash, it's very, very difficult to talk about it for a lot of men. Now, some lads are in touch with all this, and they can't stop talking about it and will do so even in public places, and that's brilliant. But the rest of us want somewhere quiet and confidential.

Some people say, 'Oh, a pub is the place to talk.' No it isn't. There's loads of people around, people are giving it bravado, leaning up against the bar, shouting and you could be interrupted at any moment. Now, I suppose when pubs were all-male affairs, it might have come up after the fifth pint, but I don't think that is really the kind of conversation anyone wants. So I really think the pub doesn't give you the nice safe feeling when you really need to share the fact that you've got three balls, and you need some advice about what to do.

A shed, on the other hand, is a mellow and controlled environment, and there's no room for bravado in a shed. The people who come into a shed with bravado are offered the stool; they're not offered the nice comfy seat. But when you're offered a comfy seat, and you chill out, that's when you might actually go, 'I tell you what, Dave, my knob's got a kink in it and I don't know why, it's just sort of rotted.'

The bottom line is that the shed is a safe place to talk about that stuff, because the shed code means your mate isn't going to break that confidence, which he might do, accidentally of course, if he was in a pub with a couple of beers inside him.

So that's one side of it, but the other side is, emotionally, you're all much more at peace in a shed than you would be in a pub. I mean, it's not about the alcohol – have a beer or something in the shed, by all means. The point is, we're talking about a shed to be a safe place to share one's innermost thoughts as a human being and as a man. That is why, spiritually, the shed is a key place. It's the place where you seek advice, yeah?

You know, the sitting room is not the place where you go, 'Hey, Derek, I've got to tell someone, man, cos I'm going mad with guilt, but I can't have sex with my wife at the moment because I went to Thailand last week and I think I might have brought home more than memories, know what I mean?' But you can say it in a shed, and you don't need a lock on the door either because the shed has its own force field which cannot be violated.

Health issues for men are very difficult to talk about. It's stuff that we don't want to confront. I mean, I'm speaking for me. I don't want to confront it, I don't want to know. I find it very difficult to talk about those kinds of things because I really don't want to go and take any action, I'd just rather be left alone. Unfortunately, though, if you do just refuse to go there, like most men, it can take you down, and I mean all the way down. So men are learning that we have to go there, but if I am going to go there, I want to be sure about who I'm divulging my deepest darkest secrets to.

I feel pretty safe bringing that stuff into the community of the shed because the selection process is intense to get into another bloke's shed. If you're having a get-together of your mates in the shed, they've gone through a huge amount of screening. Like, there are no plus-ones in a shed. You are invited as you and if you are going to bring a friend, you have to ring up and go, 'I'm bringing Sam, he's a hippy but he's really on par, he's on schedule. We know he's all right, trust me.' And even then, it may be, 'No, you're all right, mate, just come yourself. We're just having a get-together, the boys.'

So, anyone in a shed is all right. They really have been screened hard, so consequently the conversations in the shed are much more poignant and much more emotional and much more trusting, purely because everyone knows you've screened out the pirates.

At the pub, they don't screen for pirates. In fact, some people like having the pirates around in the pub, or any other social setting, because maybe they have funny stories, or they buy everyone drinks and can do a good impression of David Niven, which is all well and fine, but the trouble with bringing the pirates to the shed is that they don't understand it's sacred, even if you tell them it is, and they will talk about something that you've talked about in the shed to somebody else. So, if you are saying, 'Crikey mate, I've got a wart on the end of my knob,' you could then be in the pub three weeks later and hear, 'Hey Henry! Derek's mate told me that you've got a wart on your knob.' 'You what? Shouldn't have let that pirate in my shed.'

A lot of people imagine sheds to be lonely places, when actually the opposite is true. You do indeed spend most of your time in there alone, but you're engaged in your endeavour, which is not a lonely place to be, in fact you feel absolutely part of the brotherhood of shed dwellers. And when you do physically invite someone, who's passed the screening process, into your shed, you might think he's just going to help you fix the new race pipe on your Kawasaki, but you'll end up talking about the most intimate mental and spiritual issues you might have.

And so consequently the shed becomes a temple for male spiritual engagement. Where actually, instead of praying to a higher power, you're talking to someone who's going to answer back, but because it's all enveloped in the safe parameters of the shed, it gives you the ability to learn more about yourself or to be helped in some way.

We all hear the most awful stories about people, sometimes very successful or very famous, who can't get help, and sometimes when I hear about these tragedies I wonder if they would have been able to open up in a different context, if someone had said, 'Look, come by the shed next week, I'll show you how to change the indicator bulb on your car so it stops ticking, and we can have a cup of tea.' I just think there's a lot of people out there who would benefit from some shed time, especially with everything that's going on in the world right now. There's something about the environment of a shed that helps people drop their guard and just be themselves.

But with that all said, sometimes just chatting over your ill-health with your shed mates ain't gonna be enough to save you. And you could be headed for the big shed in the sky. And if that's going to happen, where would you want to croak? I suppose most people would say. 'In bed', which would rule out a shed, because then you've got to be in your bed and we've already established you can't have a bed in the shed (Commandment Five). But if you're going to go with your boots on, then I think a shed is a good place to make like Elvis.

Of course, the shed force field means it may be some time till your corpse is discovered. 'Where's Henry?' 'In his shed. He went over there three weeks ago and hasn't come out yet.' 'Are you gonna check on him?' 'No, I'm not allowed in there.' 'It's been three weeks, I think you are now.'

After three weeks, the great thing about sheds is you'll rot through the floor and become one with your shed. A concrete floor really is rubbish to die on, which is yet another reason to make your shed out of lovely snuggly wood.

I think a shed death wouldn't be the worst. I mean, if you are going to go, then having a coronary sitting on your Chesterfield, with a cup of tea in your hand, looking at a

Classic Bike mag, well, happy days. It also means the wife can call the undertakers and she don't have to let them come in the house. Another advantage to dying in the shed, if you're a fat lad, is that you've probably got double doors on the shed so they can get you out easily. You know, if you're a corpse in a shed, really, you've just got to be lobbed onto a stretcher and be taken out to your private ambulance. You're not going to mess up the carpet and the wife won't feel compelled to ask the ambulance people whether they want a cup of tea or anything.

There's not much to clear up in the shed, and if your wife really hated the shed, she could just set fire to it and then she's got rid of all your annoying bits and bobs as well. I think, honestly, it is better to make a funeral pyre out of the shed for the committed shed dweller on the occasion of his death, because to fill it up with the wife's BaByliss foot spas and old jam jars would be sacrilege. I was watching a documentary the other day in which they said it'll take ten years for nature to reclaim the motorways, and I thought, if I die, how long will it take for my wife to reclaim the shed and put a load of junk in it? Not ten years. It's going to take ten weeks, isn't it? Until my sheds are full of old crockery and exercise bikes, isn't it?

I do genuinely think burning a shed down when it's no longer in use is completely valid, because there is nothing more forlorn than an abandoned shed. The minute a shed doesn't have a keeper, and isn't being used, it falls into disrepair. A shed needs constant maintenance and love or it's gone.

23:
Life in the Peak Shed Era

My mates Tris and Pam gave me a little booklet the other day which they found when they were clearing out the attic. It's called, 'How to Build Garages and Sheds' and it dates from 1962.

The front cover shows a fella up a step ladder and his missus is pouring some kind of render out of a bucket for him. It's got incredibly technical information about brick-laying and in one of the pictures there's a man in a bowler hat, pulling into his newly built garage. He's closing the door on the garage he built.

The text says, 'As more and more householders become car owners, they're faced with the problem of finding parking in a garage for their cars. If you have the space, there's nothing to stop you building a garage. This should be well within your capacity after you've tried some of the simple examples described earlier in the book. What is more, it will be well worth the cost if you decide to sell your house at a later date. Building a new garage is a form of construction for which permission is required from the local by-law authority. You will probably have no difficulty in getting the permission, but you must have it, otherwise you may be served with an enforcement notice telling you to take it down.'

Well, I just find it amazing that in 1962, this bloke here, with his bowler hat on, and his little beautiful briefcase with two straps on it, a bank manager basically, could build a shed. But back then he could and he did. I mean, the absurdity of the idea that a guy like that in today's world would be interested in laying bricks and building a shed just shows how much we've lost as a society in the intervening years. That guy today would not have a clue where to even buy a brick. And there he is, in 1962, in his Vauxhall Viva, at the forefront of the information revolution.

We've lost so much in the rush forward into the modernity of life. No one's going to be capable of building a brick shed at the weekends any more, like that bloke! The middle class don't like getting their hands dirty unless it's something they've read in a wellness book or a style magazine. In that case, if they have read that you should build a shed, just underneath how to make your bruschetta on toast, then they'll go, 'Right, let's build a shed. This is the way we should do it. Come on India, come on Theodore, let's go into the garden.' Two hours later: 'Oh, darling, it's a bit cold, do you want to go in, Theo? Yes, okay. Oh, well we'll get Darryl to come round, he can finish the shed, can't he?'

That's how it is these days. But you see, back in the fifties/sixties, Mr Bank Manager, like that guy, he's going to build his own shed, isn't he? And the idea of paying a minion to do it for him wouldn't even arise. And also, not only is he going to build it, he's going to build it from scratch, to his own design, he's going to mix the concrete, he's going to lay the bricks, he's going to hammer in the rafters. And look how happy he is! Isn't that better than cooking a few vol-au-vents with cream, mushroom and bacon filling?

I mean, really, what has happened to us? How did we become so pathetic and useless? This is what shed people like me think. We think people should still be aspiring to have the skills to be able to build their own sheds, rather than playing Xbox. Building your own shed! What could be more amazing!

In that 1962 booklet, there is another picture of his beautiful big car going up to the most enormous shed that I've ever seen, and I know from that picture that he has built it that big so he can get in and out on both sides and he's got a workshop at the end where he can do his own repairs on the car. You build a shed like that and you're in ruddy clover, because you can wander around and get to every part of it. He's got his workbench, he has got his spare parts and it is just so beautiful that in this book, a shed was an aspiration of the middle classes.

Well, the middle classes now want to eat quinoa and good luck to them, I hope it brings them great happiness and long life, and maybe less and less people are wanting what I want, but I want a car and a shed and some space to tinker on it.

I get it; who needs a shed when you've got a mobile phone? Well, let me answer that by asking another question: who needs a life if you've got a mobile phone? Yes, the mobile phone is to blame for a lack of sheddery, and the rise of the mobile phone does coincide perfectly with the fall of the shed. But what is more spiritually appealing? What is better for you and your family? A shed or a mobile phone? A shed. All the way, man. It's got to be.

I'd probably have been quite happy living in the 1950s, or indeed the 1920s. The only slight problem is that I'd be dead without the NHS of today due to my diabetes, so I know it's a bit of a case of wanting to have my cake and insulin too (and with the new insulin today, I can actually do that). But looking back at the fifties and the sixties, and just allowing yourself to look at it with rose-tinted spectacles for a moment, it was all the stuff in that booklet, that was what was so magical about it. No guilt, just get on, you build your shed. You maybe go and ask the council if you can do it, and they're going to say yes, and it's not going to be a problem, because it's a free country, you know?

Now look, I'm not an idiot and I'm not ignorant of history, and I know the fifties was a tough time. I know rationing only ended in 1954. It was all post-war hardship, austerity everywhere and a lot of poverty, but the reason a lot of people like me look back on it with the old rosy specs is because you were an individual then. You weren't a number. Right? So, consequently they would call you Mr Cole at the fish shop. You could go into an ironmonger's and choose your ratchets and all that kind of stuff. You would be treated like a customer should be treated, generally.

And because there wasn't this mass-production, if you wanted to create your own shed you had to build it yourself. Cars were actually built to be serviced by their owners, not to be money-making schemes for the garages. You could balance the carbs on your Triumph, you could fix pretty well anything by the side of the road, and you didn't need a laptop computer unless you were planning the moon landing.

When it came to automotive matters, you absolutely had to 'know thy beast', whether that was a car or a motorbike. There was no self-parking or parking bleepers. There was the Haynes manual, but there was no laptop to tell you how many ding dongs and whatsits you were missing and what's gone wrong with your car. There was no one to help you really. The local garage was available, but more in a support role function; the garage's purpose was to supply the owner with the parts to enable him to do it himself when it came to servicing a vehicle.

You had to be the vessel of a certain amount of mechanical ingenuity, and no one doubted that anyone could pick it up. Even the Queen worked fixing trucks in the 1940s, and it's not fair to say that Kate Middleton's useless because she can't change a fan belt on her Land Rover because, even if she did, the thing wouldn't start up again until Mr Landrover had been by with his laptop. That ingenuity that was instilled into everyone who either owned, or knew someone who owned, a vehicle, translated into extraordinary proficiency in the shed.

Cars were not exactly simple, but they were fathomable, and shed dwellers crave, above all, the days when things just made sense on their own. So shed dwellers do look back at that time with affection because it was everything we love about being free people, uncrushed by guilt.

I do find it horrifying when I meet these kids today who are so far removed from that tradition that they don't actually know how to wire a plug. In the fifties, people were obsessed with electricity. It was the Internet of its day and not knowing how to wire a plug back then would have been as unimaginable as not knowing how to send an email today. Everybody knew how to wire stuff. They were all hands-on in the fifties, and even in the seventies and eighties people could still fix basic stuff themselves and keep stuff going. They had the expertise.

When we were kids there was *The A-Team* and there was *MacGyver*, and these shows were basically about shed dwellers who could hop into a lift at the bottom of a building and drive out on the 40th floor having converted it into an armoured car firing lift buttons with lethal force (OK, non-lethal, cos no one ever died). I don't know when being able to fix stuff and make stuff stopped being cool. MacGyver was a lunatic, and the guys in the A-Team I loved, because they did create the craziest vehicles possible out of, basically, cardboard (although I wouldn't have been seen dead in BA's van, I have to say).

I mean, I heard about one of my friend's kids recently who had no electricity in his apartment for three days because he didn't know how to push up the switch on the fuseboard. His mum had to go and do it for him (and she did, which is half of the problem). In 1970, nobody was going to come round. Nobody was going to come round and reset your trip switch for you.

And under that duress, satisfaction comes to the fore when

you have actually rewired the plug. Or you have sorted out the record player, or you have worked out how to get the shed warm with a paraffin heater. So, yes, I'd have loved to have lived in the twenties, thirties or fifties on the proviso that I was alive, as noted above.

All this talk of nostalgia for bygone days brings me onto a related point – the heritage of British industry. I'm all for the recycle, you know me. Buy it cheap, do it up, sell it on. But when all's said and done, I think there is a duty for all British shed dwellers, if they can afford one, to buy an Aston Martin, a Morgan, a Rolls-Royce or a Bentley for two major reasons: one, they are the most beautiful supercars in the world, period; two, they are built by some of the finest craftsmen and women in the world, who happen to be British. And anyone who demeans or criticizes British engineering is no friend of mine and may not come into my shed.

This country has produced, and was the instigator of, some of the greatest motorcycle and car brands in the world, and some of them are still here and they're still happening. Look at Triumph. Look at Aston. Look at Bentley. Look at Morgan. People in sheds who can afford it have a duty, as far as I am concerned, to support our British car and motorcycle industry.

If everyone decided 'Oh, I couldn't be seen in an Aston' or, 'I don't want an Aston, even though I could afford to make the payments,' then the business would be finished. There would be no business. And all those great craftsmen and women would be out of a job.

Aston Martin at the moment are embarking on building twenty-five DB5s, right, with *Goldfinger* spec, so they've got the machine guns – fake ones, don't worry – and the oil slick machine. They've got the ejector seat and the radar and all this kind of stuff. They've got it all in the car, right? You can buy the exact *Goldfinger* replica. Right? And they're 3.3 million quid each and if you can buy one you damn well should. I was at the Aston Martin works recently talking to them about it and you see those Zagatos they've just made. It moves your soul. It does something to you.

The Aston Martin Works in Newport Pagnell was where Aston Martins originally were made, and they are still there, in that massive shed, expanded now and again, building these incredible cars, and that brings tears to my eyes. That's what a shed does to me. A big one, surely, but it is still shed aesthetic. They're still hand-built. Every single bit of bodywork is rolled on an English wheel, created by craftsmen, done in the same place as it always has been since 1965 or something. And to me, to walk round that place with the history of it, and with the production of cars carrying on, it's got to be great. It is awesome.

And you get the same feeling at Morgan. You can smell it, you can breathe it in; just feel British shed dwelling at its finest. That, to me, is the pinnacle of what it's all about. Somehow you walk round that place, it makes you at peace. It gives you that kind of security that life is okay, that there's something that we should be proud of, something that we should shout about, some good news about British engineering, against all odds.

That doesn't mean you have to get an Aston to have that feeling, of course not. If it moves your soul and it makes you see the world as a better place, even for a moment, it doesn't matter whether it's a grease pump or a Rolls-Royce. Just, whatever you have in your shed must imbue you with wonderful feelings of heritage, of workmanship, of being in the presence of the product of real talented hard work. And so, consequently, it matters not a jot to me whether it's a beautifully designed double-sided Royal Enfield enamel sign promoting Royal Enfield motorcycles, or it is an Aston Martin Vantage. What matters to me is what it does to you spiritually.

Physically you can touch these things, you can smell these things, you can drive these things, you can look at these things, which is wonderful. But in a shed, where it's safe and it's warm and it's cosy, you can look at these inanimate object, you know, and kind of reminisce or imagine what they've seen and what they're all about, which is our great heritage generally, and that's got to be fantastic.

I think there's too much guilt around our heritage these days. You know, we have lots to answer for about our colonial past and the scandal of how badly those guys on the *Windrush* were let down, but there's some great things about Britain too, and we need to celebrate them and support them and we can do that by actually owning a part of our heritage, our automotive heritage.

24:
Farewell,
and Don't Let
the Door Hit You
on the Way Out

If you've actually read this whole book, then I hope you will just allow me to say, from the bottom of my heart, thank you so much. I know with everything that is going on in the world that it's an incredibly difficult time for millions of people, and I'm so flattered you spent a few quid on this, or, alternatively, took the trouble to download it from a moody website.

Either way, I hope it's been worth it and maybe given you a few ideas or a few laughs. I also know that not everyone can just build themselves a shed at the drop of a hat, either because they can't afford it, or because they live in a tower block, and the council don't fancy a shed bolted onto the wall. In that case, mate, you have to go to the metaphorical shed instead.

But if you know anyone with a garden with a wooden structure in it, however humble, get in there. I don't think sheds, and everything they stand for, have ever been more important. Men need somewhere to go and do stuff. Men need somewhere to go where there is no politics, there is no guilt, there is no virus and there is no controversy. I'm not saying we need a place where we're going to go and be chauvinistic and sexist and talk trash about our wives, because that's not it at all. It's just we need a place where we can be left alone for a little while and not try and fit into some TV commercial idea of what it means to be a man that feels incredibly foreign to a lot of us, who are actually still really focused on the day-to-day grind of putting bread on the table. Of putting one foot in front of the other. Of doing the best we can. Of surviving.

We have kids and we want the planet to be there for them. We don't want to offend anyone, that's not part of our life's dream. We don't want to rule the world. We're trying to do our bit, but we're not arrogant enough to think we're going to change it. We're just regular geezers.

But there is one place where we get to be special and different, and where we can fulfil our life's dreams, or at least aspire to have some control over our lives.

It's 4m x 3m.

It's made of wood.

It's got a twenty quid heater, a workbench and a few tools.

It can change your life.

And you'll find it at the bottom of the garden.

Acknowledgements

With deepest thanks to those who've supported me along the way:

Janie & The Boys, Vivien Cole, Major Denis Cole, David & Pam Coombes, Anna & Ashley Coombes, Martha & Robbie Coombes, Tom Sykes, Hamish Rieck, Ben Tinsley, Allen Millyard, Sam Lovegrove Jonathan Conway, Guy (Skid) Willison, Jo Colson, Steve Back, Uncle Dick Redbeard, Ben Tinsley, Richard Milner, Annabelle Norton, Tommy Clarke, Jon Wood, Mick Conefrey, Bumble, Chris Stone, Pippa McCann, Luke Clayden, Pip Froud, John Warr, Hamish Millington-Drake, Emma Lambourne, Tom Whitaker, Leah Foley, Nick Sessions, Martin Perry, Elizabeth Hurley, Katie Hurley, Henry Dent Brocklehurst, William Campbell, Jeff Ford, David Sayer, Lawrence Charles-Jones, Louis Needham, Claire Bosworth, Jo Street, Mark Ashton, Matt Knight, Hannah Benson, Peter & Annie Watson-Wood, Mike Day, Clare Voyce, Claire Pickering, Roberta Ogilvy Brown, Sylvia & Fred Tidy Harris, Paul Farmer, Deaglan Bayliss, Tom Ware, Steve Coates, Mark Upham, Simon O'Brien, Mick, Editor Adam, Tom, Dino & Mandy at Image designs, Rob Holloway, Simon

Downing, Victoria Noble, Georgina Surtess, Matt Simpson, Steve Fright, Gareth Williams, Nikki Cooper, Nigel Wright, Dave & Lynn Sutton, Henry & Kathy Birtles, Alan Cathcart, Angela Mollard, Martin Chisholm, Angus MacCurrach, Callum James, Fiona Farmer, Steve Parrish, Stuart Garner, Simon Skinner, Nick Penny, Charlie & Anna Crossley-Cooke, Charlie Meynell, Nina Rieck, Patrick Edwards, Spencer & Tish Cooper, Sebastian Rich, Rupert & Torica Back, Steve Earle, Patrick Edwards, Sean Smith, Tim & Suzanne Dams, Sally Miles, Phil & Anna Ley, Stuart & Debbie McAlpine, Emma Barker, Ghislain Pascal, Tamara Beckwith, Caprice, Neil Morrissey, Peter Thorne, Angie Peppiatt, Peter Snow, Ed Booth, Charles Dean, Jacqueline Hewer, Nicki Gottlieb, Jamie Gidlow-Jackson, Ronnie Michael, Cymon Taylor, Emma Collins, Alan & Caroline Crisp, Chris and Mel Hicks, Bruce & Lizzie Tolmie -Thomson, Louise Goodman, Alan Greenspan, Charlie Grainger, Andy and Carol Harris, Ferg & Millie Mitchell, Rupert & Didi Ivey, Julie Anne Edwards, Giles and Mel Martin, Ed and Tatiana Howard, Reggie Heyworth, Caryn & Jerry Hibbert, Simon Hilton, Quinn Williams, Diana Howie, Katy Thorogood, Gary Johnstone, Richard Cox, Satmohan Panesar, Jonah Weston, Johnny Boscawen, John Claridge, Tom Ware, James Lindsay, Anna & Ali Ekin, Gerry Lisi, Philip Luff, Richard Wolfe, Max McMurdo, Harry Metcalfe, Mickey Portman, Vincent Browett, Johnny Boston, Bear, Jay Leno, Steve & Emma Rogers, Ian Cozier Simon & Caroline White, Tom Petherick, Paul & Karen Sherratt, Stuntman Richie, Watford A&E, Steph Lifely, David & Lucinda MacFarlane, Pat O'Brien, Ed Howard, Mike & Vanessa Strutt, Invercargill A&E,

Andy Swingarm Slade, Bobby Foxworth, Chad McQueen, The Ekins Family, Stephanie Quinn, Dick Shepherd, Paul Hustler, Anthony Wallersteiner, Andrew Nott, Tony Hutchinson, Marianne Leah, Brent Jackson, Nanna & Ziggi Bollason, Amanda Rolls, Amanda Barker, William Roberts, Chris & Rachel Walker, Lord Sugar, Robert & Claudia Marsden-Smedley, Lizzie & Henry Pitman, Richard Sunderland, Simon Hawkins, Tim Frewer, Ken German, Mark & Gerry Chauveau, Gabe Chauveau, Gontze Mmutle, Amanda Byram, Johnny Peters, Rick Aplin, Ed Tudor Pole, Kate Plantin, Patrick & Ferrylyn Folkes, Nick Laughton, Sam Hardy, Anthony Jeffs, Alex Menzies, Zai Bennett, Dan Korn, Paul Welling, Paul Pascoe, Alice Beer, Gary Pinchin, Dan Sager, John & Karen Holloway, Dr Johnny Uden, Luke Brackenbury, Nigel & Louise Johnson, Anne & Rob Burchell, Paul Bader, John Sergeant, Jimmy & Sofia Watson, Paul King, Bill Wykeham, Tom Lywood, Charlie Gladstone, Phil Stone, Paul Young, Simon Schwerdt and anyone else I've forgotten!